UNLOCKING
AP® U.S. GOVERNMENT

Answer Key

Larry G. Harmon, Ph.D.

Unlocking AP® U.S. Government
is one of a series of AP® test preparation books

© **2018 Harmon Publishing**

Preface

The idea for this guide generated from the College Board's redesign of the AP Government and Politics course and the success of my publication *Unlocking AP U.S. History* in helping students qualify for college credit. Students experience great results on the AP exam when they have access to an annotated Curriculum Framework, with content relevant to the test. And they understand best how to write successfully when they are provided many examples of FRQs aligned to the curriculum and answer keys that score every point on the AP rubrics. Specifically, students ask: what must I write and what does a great answer look like? Show me, don't tell me.

Unlocking AP U.S. Government and Politics provides the **ANSWER KEYS!** It is the only AP Test Preparation book on the market that:

1. **Annotates the AP Curriculum Framework**. The content students must know for the multiple-choice exam is based on an outline published by the College Board. The outline is called the Curriculum Framework and is provided in this review book. Unlocking AP U.S. Government annotates the Framework to provide students the key vocabulary and concepts that appear on the AP U.S. Government exam.

2. Provides a one-page brief for each of the **15 required Supreme Court cases**. Each brief includes the constitutional issue, the judicial question, the background of the case, and the Supreme Court holding and reasoning

3. Provides a one-page summary of the main ideas for each of the required **Foundational Documents** and excerpts that will appear on the AP exam.

4. Provides **Free-Response Questions** aligned to the Curriculum Framework **and exemplary answers** for each of the four types of FRQs that will appear on the AP exam. The answers score every point on the AP rubric.

Acknowledgments

In writing this guide, I am indebted to many educators and students. Their insights, questions, and willingness to experiment in the spirit of improvement were invaluable.

My former and present students have been a constant source of inspiration. Many served as knowing experimenters and gave helpful feedback so that the model is student-centered.

My family encouraged my career in education and specifically demanded that I write the guidebook for AP teachers and students. To qualify for college credit while in high school is a great personal accomplishment for a student and a special honor and loving respect for one's parents and guardians. To the students studying AP Government and Politics, your efforts do reap rewards.

Larry Harmon, Ph.D.
July 2018

About the Author

Larry G. Harmon received his B.A. in History, an M.S. in Secondary Education, and a Ph.D. in Curriculum and Instruction from the University of North Texas. He has served in the Texas public schools as a teacher, Executive Director of Curriculum and Instruction, and High School principal for more than 25 years. He re-entered public education to teach AP U.S. Government and Politics at Mansfield High School in Mansfield, Texas.

Titles in the Unlocking AP Series

Unlocking the AP U.S. History Exam
Unlocking the AP World History Exam
Unlocking the AP Government Exam

CONTENTS

Qualifying for College Credit: Question and Answer

Q: How do I earn a three or higher on the AP U.S. Government Exam?

A: In general, students earn a "3" on the exam when their scores place them in the top half of all students taking the AP test. More than 320,000 students take the AP U.S. Government and Politics exam every spring. Generally, students earn a "4" on the exam by placing in the top 25% and earn a "5" by placing in the top 10%.

Q: What is the format of the test and how much time to I have for each part?

A: The AP U.S. Government exam is divided into four sections with a total exam time of 3 hours and 15 minutes. The table below describes the four sections.

Section	Length	Time	% of Score
1. Multiple-Choice	55 questions	1 hour and 20 minutes	50%
2. Free Response	4 questions	1 hour and 40 minutes	50%
• Concept Application		20 minutes	12.5%
• Qualitative Analysis		20 minutes	12.5%
• SCOTUS Comparison		20 minutes	12.5%
• Argument Essay		40 minutes	12.5%

Q: I don't feel prepared to do well on the AP exam. How should I study if I have only two weeks before the test?

A: The most effective study involves reviewing content by unit. The AP U.S. Government exam is divided into five thematic units. Each unit will be assessed on the multiple-choice and free-response sections of the exam. Here is a good review plan:

Time	Content to Study	Skills to Practice
Day One	Unit 1: Foundations of American Democracy	Memorize the main ideas of the required Foundational Documents and be able to apply them in political scenarios. Remember, you must be able to use at least one required document to support the thesis of your argumentative essay. Six of the Nine required documents are based on Unit One.
Day Two	Unit 2: Interactions Among Branches of Government	Memorize the main ideas of the 2 Foundational Documents in this unit and be able to apply them in political scenarios. Memorize the constitutional issues, background and holdings of the 3 required Supreme Court decisions in this unit.
Day Three	Period 3: Civil Liberties and Civil Rights	Memorize the constitutional issues, background and holdings of the 10 required Supreme Court decisions in this unit. Be prepared to explain the effect of the holding on the actions of the three branches of government or a linkage institution.
Day Four	Period 4: American Political Ideologies and Beliefs	Be able to analyze political data (chart, graphs, tables, polls) in order to: • Describe a pattern or trend • Draw a conclusion about the pattern or trend • Explain what the data implies about one of the major themes of the course.
Day Five	Period 5: Political Participation (Linkage Institutions)	Prepare to write about how each of the four linkage institutions connect the citizenry to their government.

The plan for Days 6–10? Repeat Days One through Five! You must build mastery of the content so you are confident writing about it.

Unlocking the Multiple-Choice Exam

Every question on the multiple-choice exam is based on one of the "big ideas" recorded on the AP Curriculum Framework. The format of the AP U.S. Government Framework is an outline based on the five units of the course and is provided for you in this book.

Notice that the Framework is divided into three parts: 1) an Enduring Understanding (this is where the Free Response Questions originate); 2) Learning Objectives labelled as A, B, C, etc. (this is where the multiple-choice questions originate) and; 3) Essential Knowledge labelled 1, 2, 3, etc. (this is the source of the multiple-choice answers).

Prepare for the multiple-choice exam by:

1. **Reading the Curriculum Framework outline.** Notice the document has been annotated with commentary, tables, and bulleted lists, and graphics. This evidence is eligible to be tested as part of the multiple-choice questions.

2. **Studying the definitions of key terms and mostly importantly, their significance on the name of the unit.** The AP multiple-choice test measures your knowledge of government and politics with only 55 questions. Therefore, most of the questions assess broad ideas and political significance, not merely definitions of terms.

3. About half of the multiple-choice questions are anchored to a "stimulus" – a short reading passage, quote, map, graph, cartoon, or chart. The information in the stimulus supports only one answer choice. For the most difficult questions, when you have eliminated the options down to two answers, remember that **only one answer choice is supported by the stimulus. The second answer choice may be an accurate statement of U.S. Government, but it is not supported by the evidence provided.**

Unlocking Free-Response Question 1: Concept Application

The Concept Application question will be based on a scenario described in approximately 150 words. Each part of the question (A), (B), and (C) relates to the scenario. Overall, this question is worth three points. To earn a perfect score, your response must do the following:

Part A: (1 point) In several sentences, **describe a political institution, behavior, or process connected with the scenario.**

Part B: (1 point) In several sentences, **explain how your response in Part (A) could be affected by a political process, government entity, or citizen behavior** provided in the prompt. This FRQ requires students to connect the scenario to different aspects of the course; for example, relate the scenario to different branches of government, or linkage institutions, or different political ideologies.

Part C: (1 point) In several sentences, **explain how the scenario relates to another political process, government entity, or citizen behavior.**

Unlocking Free-Response Question 2: Quantitative Analysis

The Quantitative Analysis question is divided into three parts: (A), (B), and (C). Overall, this question is worth four points. To earn a perfect score, your response must do the following:

Part A: (1 point) Identify or **describe the data** in the quantitative visual. This requires a one-sentence response.

Part B: (1ˢᵗ point) In a couple of sentences, **describe a pattern, trend, or similarity/difference** as required in the question. If the stimulus is a chart or graph, the trend will be either a positive relationship, negative relationship or no relationship between the two variables.

Part B: (2ⁿᵈ point) In a couple of sentences, **draw a conclusion for that pattern, trend, or similarity/difference.** You may want to start that sentence with "One can conclude that …"

Part C: (1 point) In several sentences, **explain how specific data in the visual demonstrates a principle** in the prompt. Common principles include: federalism, limited government, popular sovereignty, participatory democracy, pluralism, checks and balances, partisanship, divided government, judicial review, and political socialization.

Unlocking Free-Response Question 3: SCOTUS Comparison

The Supreme Court comparison is divided into three parts: (A), (B), and (C). Overall, this question is worth four points. To earn a perfect score, your response must do the following:

Part A: (1 point) Identify the **constitutional clause** that is common to both cases. This requires a one-sentence response.

Part B: (1ˢᵗ point) Provide **factual information about the required Supreme Court case.** This case will be one of the 15 you studied and briefed in class. In a couple of sentences, describe the holding of this case and how it relates to the constitutional issue.

Part B: (2ⁿᵈ point) In a couple of sentences, explain **how the information from the required case is relevant to the non-required case** described in the question. You will either describe how the cases are similar or different.

Part C: (1 point) In a couple of sentences, **explain an interaction** between the holding of the non-required case and the political institution or process mentioned in the question. This part of the FRQ is asking you to extend the facts of the case to a follow-up scenario.

Unlocking Free-Response Question 4: Argumentative Essay

The Argumentative Essay is worth six points. To earn a perfect score, your essay response must do the following:

1 point: Write a defensible **thesis** that responds to the question and addresses two lines of reasoning. The essay can begin with the thesis statement. No points awarded for introductory sentences.

2 points: Describe ONE piece of **specific evidence** that supports your thesis. You will be given a list of three foundational documents. Choose one, describe its main idea, and connect that main idea to your thesis statement. One of the three foundational documents will be the U.S. Constitution. The important aspects of the Constitution that would most likely connect to your FRQ prompt are: commerce clause, due process clause, equal protection clause, 10th Amendment (reserved powers to the states and people), and judicial review.

1 point: Describe A SECOND piece of **specific evidence** that supports your thesis.

1 point: Use **reasoning** to explain why or how the evidence supports the thesis. This point is earned by explaining why your evidence is significance. Naturally, you will explain the significance after you have described one of your pieces of evidence. You may want to start this sentence with "This evidence shows that ...."

1 point: Provide an **alternative perspective** using refutation concession, or rebuttal. Address this requirement as the last paragraph of your essay. You may want to start the first sentence with "Other political scientists would argue that ..."

UNIT 1: FOUNDATIONS OF AMERICAN DEMOCRACY

Enduring Understanding LIBERTY AND ORDER-1: A balance between governmental power and individual rights has been a hallmark of American political development.

A. Explain how democratic ideals are reflected in the Declaration of Independence and the U.S. Constitution.

1. The U.S. government is based on the ideas of limited government, including natural rights, popular sovereignty, republicanism, and social contract.

   - **Limited government:** A principle of constitutional government; a government whose powers are defined and limited by a constitution. Also based on the principle of "rule of law" – laws apply to everyone, even those who govern.
   - **Popular sovereignty:** a government based on the consent of the people rule. The government's source of authority is the people, and its power is not legitimate if it disregards the will of the people. A government established by the free choice of the people is expected to serve the people, who hold sovereignty, or supreme power.
   - **Republicanism:** A philosophy of limited government with elected representatives serving at the will of the people. The government is based on consent of the governed.
   - **Social contract:** English philosopher John Locke advocated the idea of a "social contract" in which government powers are derived from the consent of the governed and in which the government serves the people. The social contract in the U.S. is the agreement by which people define their individual rights and elected representatives uphold them.

- **Natural Rights:** rights inherent in human beings, not dependent on governments, which include life, liberty, and property. The concept of natural rights was central to English philosopher John Locke's theories about government and was widely accepted among America's founding fathers.

2. The **Declaration of Independence**, drafted by Jefferson, with help from Adams and Franklin, provides a foundation for popular sovereignty, while the **U.S. Constitution** drafted at the Philadelphia convention provides the blueprint for a unique form of political democracy in the U.S.

   - **Popular sovereignty addressed in the Declaration of Independence**: governments are those "deriving their just Powers from the Consent of the Governed."

   - **Popular sovereignty addressed in the U.S. Constitution**
     - "The people" were involved either directly or through their representatives in the making and the ratification of the Constitution.
     - The framers of the Constitution proclaimed popular sovereignty in the Preamble: "We the people of the United States ... do ordain and establish this Constitution for the United States of America."
     - The people are involved directly or indirectly in proposing and ratifying amendments to their constitution. Article VII of the Constitution requires the people in nine states approve the proposed framework of government before it replaced the Articles of Confederation.
     - The people indicate support for their government when they vote in public elections and work to influence public policy decisions and otherwise encourage their representatives in government to be accountable to them. Article I of the Constitution requires members of the House of Representatives to be elected directly by the people. The 17th Amendment made U.S. Senators directly elected by the people.

B. Explain how models of representative democracy are visible in major institutions, policies, events, or debates in the U.S.

1. Representative democracies can take several forms along this scale: participatory democracy, pluralist democracy, and elite democracy.

Model of Representative Democracy	Key Features
Participatory democracy emphasizes broad participation in politics and civil society; a democracy which is conducted by people's active or direct participation.	<ul><li>Voting in elections</li><li>Organizing petitions, assemblies, interest groups, and political parties.</li><li>Funding candidates for election</li><li>Decision-making by majority vote</li><li>Emphasis on political equality, especially individual liberties.</li></ul>
Pluralist democracy recognizes group-based activism by nongovernmental interests striving to impact on political decision making. Political power is distributed among many groups like-minded people, unions, professional associations and business lobbyists. Pluralists believe that: <ul><li>Power is fragmented.</li><li>Groups provide a more effective means of representation.</li><li>The larger the group the more influence it will have.</li><li>Policies are established through bargaining and compromise and tend to be fair to all in the end.</li></ul>	**Insider groups** are well established and able to work closely with the elected officials in government because of their position or prestige within the community. Example: professional groups that have lobbying associations to promote the interests of their members. **Outsider groups** have less access to elected officials. Examples of these groups include: <ul><li>Grassroots activists that hold marches and rallies to bring attention or action for their cause.</li><li>Political Action Committees (PACs) that collect and distribute money to support specific candidates for office.</li></ul>
Elite democracy emphasizes limited participation in politics and civil society. It claims that a single elite, not many competing groups, decides the critical issues for the nation, leaving minor matters for the middle level and almost nothing for the common person.	The elite draws its members from three areas: the highest political leaders including the president and close advisers; major corporate owners and directors; and high-ranking military officers. For the most part, the elite respects civil liberties, follows established constitutional principles, and operates openly and peacefully. Their influence can be seen through the power of iron triangles and campaign-finance (Super PACs, 501(c)(4)s, and think tanks).

2. Different aspects of the U.S. Constitution, as well as the debate between the **Federalist No. 10** and **Brutus No. 1**, reflect the tension between the broad participatory model and the more filtered participation of the pluralist and elite models.

Foundation Document: Brutus 1

Background: Since its inception, the United States has sought to balance government power and individual rights. The Declaration of Independence, Brutus 1, Federalist 10 describe the difficulties of establishing good government. The Anti-Federalists considered the Constitution to be a class-based document intended to ensure that a particular economic elite controlled the new government, and they believed that the Constitution would weaken the power of the states. When the new Constitution was proposed for ratification, an Antifederalists, writing under the alias Brutus, raised this concern: Could a large and growing republic with a diverse people be united under one government without sacrificing the blessings of liberty?

Main Ideas of Brutus 1 and Critical Passages
• **Citizens must be cautious about empowering a strong central government because they are unlikely to ever get control back.**
"Remember, when the people once part with power, they can seldom or never resume it again but by force. Many instances can be produced in which the people have voluntarily increased the powers of their rulers; but few, if any, in which rulers have willingly abridged their authority."
• **The new constitution gives so much power to a central government that the state governments may no longer be able to function. The "necessary and proper" clause and the supremacy clause make the central government an uncontrollable power.**
"Although the government reported by the convention does not go to a perfect and entire consolidation, yet it approaches so near to it, that it must, if executed, certainly and infallibly terminate in it.... This government is to possess absolute and uncontrollable power, legislative, executive and judicial, with respect to every object to which it extends... And by the 6th article, it is declared that this constitution shall be the supreme law of the land.... It appears from these articles that ... the constitution and laws of every state are nullified and declared void, so far as they are or shall be inconsistent with this constitution.... The government then ... is a complete one.
• **There is no limit to Congress' power to tax because it decides what is meant by "common defense" and "general welfare." Taxation allows the central government to extend control over every facet of the nation.**
"The legislative power is competent to lay taxes, duties, imposts, and excises; —there is no limitation to this power, ... but the legislature have authority to contract debts at their discretion; they are the sole judges of what is necessary to provide for the common defense, and they only are to determine what is for the general welfare; this power therefore is neither more nor less, than a power to lay and collect taxes, imposts, and excises, at their pleasure; not only [is] the power to lay taxes unlimited, as to the amount they may require, but it is perfect and absolute to raise them in any mode they please.... No state can emit paper money—lay any duties, or imposts, on imports, or exports, but by consent of the Congress; and then the net produce shall be for the benefit of the United States."

Main Ideas of Brutus 1 and Critical Passages

- **The federal courts, in time, will destroy the state courts.**

"The judicial power of the United States is to be vested in a supreme court, and in such inferior courts as Congress may from time to time ordain and establish. These courts will be, in themselves, totally independent of the states, deriving their authority from the United States, and receiving from them fixed salaries; and in the course of human events it is to be expected, that they will swallow up all the powers of the courts in the respective states."

- **In such a large republic, it will be too hard for the representatives to understand the will of the people.**

"a free republic cannot succeed over a country of such immense extent, containing such a number of inhabitants, and these increasing in such rapid progression as that of the whole United States.... In a large republic, the public good is sacrificed to a thousand views; it is subordinate to exceptions, and depends on accidents. In a small one, the interest of the public is easier perceived, better understood, and more within the reach of every citizen; abuses are of less extent, and of course are less protected."

- **A large republic will create a class of elected officials who will abuse their power and enrich themselves and their friends.**

"In so extensive a republic, the great officers of government would soon become above the control of the people, and abuse their power to the purpose of aggrandizing themselves, and oppressing them...The command of all the troops and navy of the republic, the appointment of officers, the power of pardoning offences, the collecting of all the public revenues, and the power of expending them, with a number of other powers, must be lodged and exercised in every state, in the hands of a few.... They will use the power, when they have acquired it, to the purposes of gratifying their own interest and ambition, and it is scarcely possible, in a very large republic, to call them to account for their misconduct, or to prevent their abuse of power.

Brutus 1 argues that the U.S. Constitution will create a central government controlled by an elite of elected representatives who have the power to destroy the sovereignty of the states. By the power to tax, declare supremacy over state laws, control a national military, print a national currency, borrow against the wealth of the citizens, and determine what is in the "general welfare" of the nation, a central government allows elites the strategies to control the fate of the nation. The best remedy against an elitist model of representative government is a system that retains strong state sovereignty. People have a greater chance of participating in a democracy through local rule where elected officials are more accessible and accountable.

Foundation Document: Federalist 10

Background: Since its inception, the United States has sought to balance government power and individual rights. The Declaration of Independence, Brutus 1, Federalist 10 describe the difficulties of establishing good government. The Federalists supported the adoption of the Constitution and published a series of essays called the *Federalist Papers*, that explained its benefits over the confederation.

Main Ideas of Federalist 10 and Critical Passages
• **A strong faction cannot tyrannize the public through superior force. The cause of factions is unequal distribution of wealth and the main task of government is to balance their interests.** "But the most common and durable source of factions has been the various and unequal distribution of property. Those who hold and those who are without property have ever formed distinct interests in society. Those who are creditors, and those who are debtors, fall under a like discrimination. A landed interest, a manufacturing interest, a mercantile interest, a moneyed interest, with many lesser interests, grow up of necessity in civilized nations, and divide them into different classes, actuated by different views. The regulation of these various and interfering interests forms the principal task of modern legislation, and involves the spirit of party and faction in the necessary operations of the government."
• **To control faction, Madison proposes a republic, which can govern a greater expanse of territory than a pure democracy. A large republic will dilute the power of factions. Leaders will be more isolated in the states, making a faction difficult to spread from state to nation.** "There are two methods of removing the causes of faction: the one, by destroying the liberty which is essential to its existence; the other, by giving to every citizen the same opinions, the same passions, and the same interests.... It could never be more truly said than of the first remedy, that it was worse than the disease. Liberty is to faction what air is to fire, an aliment without which it instantly expires. But it could not be less folly to abolish liberty, which is essential to political life, because it nourishes faction, than it would be to wish the annihilation of air, which is essential to animal life, because it imparts to fire its destructive agency.... A republic, by which I mean a government in which the scheme of representation takes place, opens a different prospect, and promises the cure for which we are seeking.... If a faction consists of less than a majority, relief is supplied by the republican principle, which enables the majority to defeat its sinister views, by regular vote. It may clog the administration, it may convulse the society; but it will be unable to execute and mask its violence under the forms of the constitution.... Extend the sphere, and you take in a greater variety of parties and interests; you make it less probable that a majority will have a common motive to invade the rights of other citizens.
Madison argues that the nature of man is to form factions based on levels of wealth. Factions are inherently opposed to the national interest and must be controlled through constitutional devices, including federalism and a large republic. Government must be designed to control and channel faction rather than prevent it. The Constitutional provisions of separation of powers, checks and balances, extraordinary majorities, and the Bill of Rights are purposely designed to prevent the easy rule of the majority.

Enduring Understanding CONSTITUTIONALISM-1: The Constitution emerged from the debate about the weaknesses in the Articles of Confederation as a blueprint for limited government.

A. Explain how Federalist and Anti-Federalist views on central government and democracy are reflected in U.S. foundational documents.

1. Madison's arguments in Federalist No. 10 focused on the superiority of a large republic in controlling the "mischiefs of faction," delegating authority to elected representative and dispersing power between the states and national government.

2. Anti-Federalist writings, including Brutus No. 1, adhered to popular democracies theory that emphasized the benefits of a small decentralized republic while warning of the dangers to personal liberty from a large, centralized government.

Commentary: The Federalists and Anti-Federalists primarily debated about the scope of power of the central government. In Federalist No. 10, Madison argued that factions (political groups/special interests) are natural but controllable by institutions of government. Separation of powers and checks and balances will limit the power of any one group or alliance of groups to dominate policy. The "Madisonian model" of government are based on these two principles. For Madison, the legislative branch was given more authority than the other two branches (especially the powers to tax, fund government operations, borrow money, and approve presidential appointments including federal judges). Separating Congress into a House of Representatives and Senate was intended to make the law-making process slow and deliberate.

The table below compares the positions of these two groups.

Federalists	Anti-Federalists
• Favored a strong central government and weak state governments • Argued that the Bill of Rights was not necessary (Congress did not have the constitutional power to deny natural rights) • Favored a separation of powers among three branches of government with checks and balances • Believed that a large republic would ensure individual freedoms	• Favored a weak central government and strong state governments • Believed the Bill of Rights was necessary to fulfill the promise of the Declaration of Independence (natural rights should be protected by government authorities) • Favored the states checking the power of the central government • Believed an American republic would grow so large it would transform, like Greece and Rome, into authoritarian system.

B. Explain the relationship between key provisions of the Articles of Confederation and the debate over granting the federal government greater power formerly reserved to the states.

1. Specific incidents and legal challenges that highlighted key weaknesses of the Articles of Confederation are represented by the table below.

Weakness of Confederation	Problem it Created	Constitutional Solution
Congress unable to levy or collect taxes	The nation could not pay off war debts, which led to Shays' Rebellion	Congress given the power to levy taxes (Article I, Section 8)
No centralized military power to address Shays' Rebellion	National government unable to defend itself or the citizens	Congress given the power to raise an army and a navy (Article I, Section 8)
Congress unable to regulate foreign and interstate commerce	States charge tariffs on each other. States banned some trade.	Congress given the power to regulate interstate commerce (Article I, Section 8)
No national court system	No methods to resolve disputes among the states. No way to try those who broke national laws.	Creation of a national court system (Article III)
Government dominated by the states	States refused to fully fund the national government.	The Constitution establishes the supremacy clause – national laws supreme over states (Article VI)

C. Explain the ongoing impact of political negotiation and compromise at the Constitutional Convention on the development of the constitutional system.
   1. Compromises deemed necessary for adoption and ratification of the **Constitution** are represented by:

---

1. **The Great Compromise: Will representation in Congress be based on the population of the states or equality among the states?**

Early in the Constitutional Convention, two Virginians revealed a manuscript that called for a national executive, a national judiciary and a two-house legislature, the lower house chosen by popular vote. In both houses, representation was to be based on population or wealth. This "Virginia Plan" was intended to guide the development of a new Constitution. And it did. But a plan from New Jersey delegates challenged Virginia's plan on representation and offered to preserve the powers of the small states on a basis of equality with their larger neighbors. A resolution offered by Connecticut delegates, called the "Great Compromise" was adopted, providing proportional representation in the House of Representatives and an equal vote for the Senate.

2. **The Three-Fifths Compromise: Will representation in Congress be balanced between free and slave states?**

A second compromise, the "three-fifths compromise" provided that three whites were to be counted equivalent to five Negroes in matters involving direct taxes and representation in the House of Representatives. The three-fifths formula was created to give the planting states of the South equal representation in the House as the commercial states of the North.

3. **The Importation of Slaves: Will the Constitution favor or discourage slavery?**

Governeur Morris of New York condemned slavery at the convention, arguing that it was a "nefarious institution." The slaveholders at the convention recognized the contradictions between slavery and republicanism but only supported an end to the slave trade and not slavery itself. Northern and southern interests negotiated an agreement that Congress would not forbid imports of slaves before 1808.

4. **Electoral College: How will the President of the United States be chosen?**

The Articles of Confederation did not provide for a Chief Executive of the United States. Therefore, when delegates decided that a president was necessary, there was a disagreement over how he should be elected to office. While some delegates felt that the president should be popularly elected, others feared that the electorate would not be informed enough to make a wide decision. They came up with other alternatives such as going through each state's Senate to elect the president. In the end, the two sides compromised with the creation of the electoral college. Thus, citizens would vote for electors who then selected the president. By common consent, George Washington was to the first executive of the new state.

---

2. Debates about self-government during the drafting of the **Constitution** necessitated the drafting of an amendment process in Article V that entailed either a two-thirds vote in both houses or a proposal from two-thirds of the state legislatures, with final ratification determined by three-fourths of the states.

Commentary: The amendment process is based on the principle of federalism, shared powers between states and the central government. The Constitution has been amended 27 times. For 26 amendments, the process included a proposal by Congress and ratification (approval) by the states.

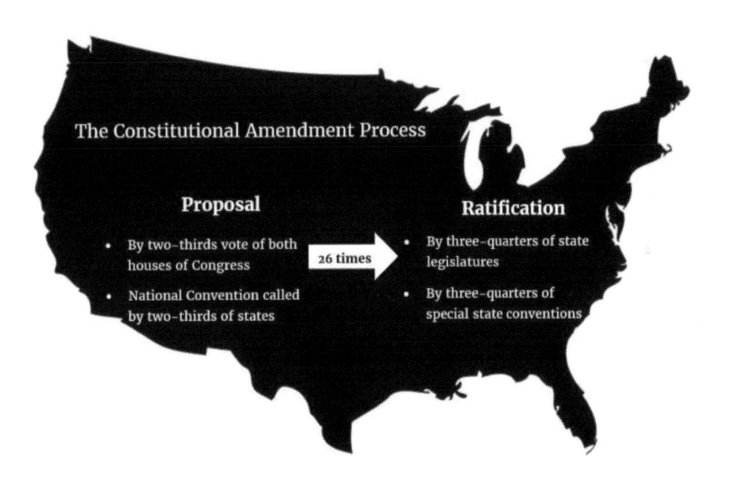

The Constitutional Amendment Process

Proposal

- By two-thirds vote of both houses of Congress

- National Convention called by two-thirds of states

26 times

Ratification

- By three-quarters of state legislatures

- By three-quarters of special state conventions

3. The compromises necessary to secure ratification of the Constitution left some matters unresolved that continue to generate discussion and debate today.

4. The debate over the role of the central government, the powers of the state governments, and the rights of individuals remains at the heart of present-day constitutional issues about democracy and governmental power, as represented by:

   • Debates about government surveillance resulting from federal government's response to the 9/11 attacks.
   • The debate about the role of the federal government in public school education.

Enduring Understanding COMPETITING POLICY-MAKING INTERESTS-1: The Constitution created a competitive policy-making process to ensure the people's will is represented and that freedom is preserved.

A. Explain the constitutional principles of separation of powers and checks and balances.

   1. The powers allocated to Congress, the president, and the courts demonstrate the separation of powers and checks and balances features of the U.S. Constitution.

Three Branches of Government

Separation of Powers and Checks and Balances

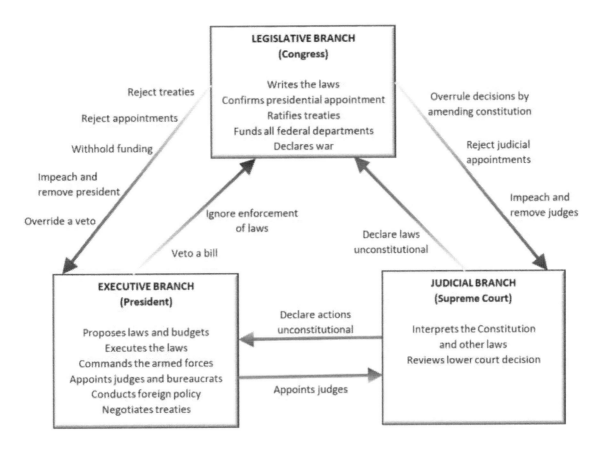

2. The Federalist No. 51 explains how constitutional provision of separation of powers and checks and balances control abuses by majorities.

    Background: James Madison understood that once a single branch of government — legislative, executive or judicial — had accumulated all political power in its hands, nothing could prevent government tyrannically. The checks and balances between the branches are essential to prevent authoritarian government. Madison shared his philosophy and observations on why human nature makes politics (sharing political power) so challenging.

Main Ideas of Federalist 51 and Critical Passages

- **A separation of federal power into three branches, with all accountable to the people will ensure democracy.**

"It is evident that each department should have a will of its own; and consequently should be so constituted, that the members of each should have as little agency as possible in the appointment of the members of the others. Were this principle rigorously adhered to, it would require that all the appointments for the supreme executive, legislative, and judiciary magistracies, should be drawn from the same fountain of authority, the people, through channels having no communication whatever with one another."

- **A system of checks and balances will prevent authoritarian control by one faction.**

"But the great security against a gradual concentration of the several powers in the same department, consists in giving to those who administer each department, the necessary constitutional means, and personal motives, to resist encroachments of the others.... Ambition must be made to counteract ambition.... If men were angels, no government would be necessary. If angels were to govern men, neither external nor internal controls on government would be necessary. In framing a government which is to be administered by men over men, the great difficulty lies in this: you must first enable the government to control the governed; and in the next place oblige it to control itself. A dependence on the people is, no doubt, the primary control on the government; but experience has taught mankind the necessity of auxiliary precautions."

- **To prevent the legislature from assuming too much power, divide it into two houses and provide the President with veto power.**

"In republican government, the legislative authority necessarily predominates. The remedy is to divide the legislature into different branches; and to render them, by different modes of election, and different principles of action, as little connected with each other, as the nature of their common functions, and their common dependence on the society, will admit.... As the weight of the legislative authority requires that it should be thus divided, the weakness of the executive may require, on the other hand, that it should be fortified. An absolute negative on the legislature, appears, at first view, to be the natural defense with which the executive magistrate should be armed."

Main Ideas of Federalist 51 and Critical Passages

- **Justice and civil society can be ensured by two methods: 1) protection of minority rights (which became the Bill of Rights) and 2) separation of powers and federalism.**

"It is of great importance in a republic, not only to guard the society against the oppression of its rulers; but to guard one part of the society against the injustice of the other part. Different interests necessarily exist in different classes of citizens. If a majority be united by a common interest, the rights of the minority will be insecure. There are but two methods of providing against this evil: the one, by creating a will in the community independent of the majority, that is, of the society itself; the other, by comprehending in the society so many separate descriptions of citizens, as will render an unjust combination of a majority of the whole very improbable, if not impracticable.... And happily for the *republican cause*, the practicable sphere may be carried to a very great extent, by a judicious modification and mixture of the *federal principle*."

Madison championed the idea of pluralist democracy. Three branches of government must be created so that each can check the power of the other two branches. Additionally, each branch of government should be dependent on the people who are the source of authority. Madison acknowledges that men are not angels and therefore those who exercise political power must be limited. When government, like society, is broken into many parts, the rights of individuals, especially minorities, will be protected from tyranny. Separation of powers and checks and balances ensures justice in a society of competitive groups. Only strong coalitions representing majority views will be able to influence policy.

---

3. The three models of representative democracy continue to be reflected in contemporary institution and political behavior.

B. Explain the implication of separation of powers and checks and balances for the U.S. political system.

1. Multiple access points for stakeholders and institutions to influence public policy flows from the separation of powers and checks and balances.

   Commentary: These access points are called linkage institutions and include:
   - Political parties: organizing a common agenda and running candidates to control government.
   - Interest Groups: organizing citizens around a narrow issue and influencing policy through lobbying, campaigning, and use of mass media and social media.
   - Media: organizing demonstrations, protests, polling, and publishing campaigns that gain public interest and regional and national media coverage.

- Elections: organizing voting blocks and transportation to the polls; campaigning; and voter registration drives.

2. Impeachment, removal, and other legal actions taken against public officials deemed to have abused their power reflect the purpose of checks and balances.

   Commentary: Congress holds the power to impeach and remove top officials from the executive branch (President, cabinet, heads of bureaucratic department) and the federal courts. The House of Representatives can <u>impeach</u> (bring a formal allegation against an official) by majority vote. Then, the Senate tries the official and can <u>remove</u> with a two-thirds vote.

Enduring Understanding CONSTITUTIONALISM-2: Federalism reflects the dynamic distribution of power between national and state governments.

A. Explain how societal needs affect the constitutional allocation of power between the national and state governments.

1. The exclusive and concurrent powers of the national and state governments help explain the negotiation over the balance of power between the two levels.

Federalism: The Division of Powers Between National and State Government

National Powers (exclusive)	Concurrent Powers (shared)	State Powers (reserved)
<ul><li>Coin Money</li><li>Regulate interstate and foreign trade</li><li>Raise and maintain armed forces</li><li>Declare war</li><li>Conduct foreign affairs</li></ul>	<ul><li>Levy taxes</li><li>Borrow money</li><li>Establish courts</li><li>Define crimes and set punishments</li><li>Eminent domain (take property for public use)</li></ul>	<ul><li>Regulate trade within the state</li><li>Establish public schools</li><li>Conduct Elections</li><li>Establish local governments</li><li>Establish license requirements for professionals</li></ul>

2. The distribution of power between federal and state governments to meet the needs of society changes, as reflected by grants, incentives, and aid programs, including federal revenue sharing, mandates, categorical grants, and block grants.

Commentary: Fiscal federalism involves spending, taxing, and providing grants in the federal system. **Grants-in-aid** are the main strategy the national government uses to aid and influence states and local governments. In 2014, federal grants to states began increasing significantly. Medicaid increases are the main source of this upward trend, while funding for other programs, such as education and transportation, is declining.

States get roughly one-third of their revenue from the federal government—funding that pays for health care, schools, roads, public safety, and a range of other programs. Federal grants to states are about 40 percent higher, after adjusting for inflation, than they were in 2008 when the recession began. But federal support for this range of programs has varied significantly, with grants for health care growing 72 percent in real terms from 2008-17, while almost all other areas saw a decrease. One factor contributing to the rise in federal health grants is the Medicaid expansion under the Affordable Care Act (Obama Care) which went into effect in 2014. **See graphs below.**

There are two major types of federal aid for states and local governments:
- **Categorical grants** are the main source of federal aid and can be used only for specific purposes (categories). State and local governments must apply for categorical grants and accept the rules and requirements that come with them, such as nondiscrimination provisions.
- **Block grants** are large sums of money granted to states to support broad programs like community development and social services. States have discretion in deciding how to spend the money.

In recent years states have been burdened by **mandates.** These actions require states to spend money to comply with a law of Congress or a federal court order. Examples include: The Clean Air Act which forces the states to comply with Environmental Protection regulations by raising taxes or cutting other spending. The Americans with Disabilities Act of 1990 required state and local governments to refit government buildings with elevators and wheelchair ramps for the immobile. These two laws are also examples of unfunded mandates, in which the federal government provided no funds for the states to comply. In 1995, Congress passed a law that will make it more difficult for Congress to impose new unfunded mandates.

Federal Grants to States
percentage change from fiscal year 2008, adjusted for inflation

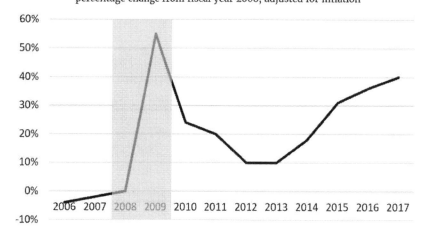

Source: The Pew Charitable Trust, 2017. The recession period is shaded.

Trends in Federal Grants to States by Program Area
percentage change from fiscal year 2008 to 2017

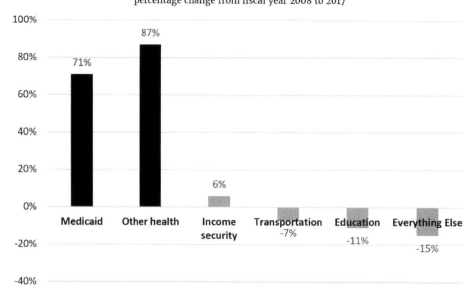

Note: "Other health" includes all items in the health budget other than Medicaid, including the Children's Health Insurance Program and grants for things like substance abuse and vaccines for children. "Everything else" includes the following budget functions: agriculture, energy, natural resources, environment, and veterans' benefits.

Source: The Pew Charitable Trust, 2017. The recession period is shaded.

B. Explain how the appropriate balance of power between national and state governments has been interpreted differently over time.

1. The interpretation of the Tenth and Fourteenth Amendments, the commerce clause, the necessary and proper clause, and other enumerated and implied powers is at the heart of the debate over the balance of power between the national and state governments.

Constitutional Provision	Effect on the balance of power
Tenth Amendment reserves to the states and the people all powers not granted the national government or prohibited to the states. Traditionally, these powers include health, education, and welfare.	This amendment is the basis of federalism and state sovereignty. It does not effectively balance power with the national government but allows states control over matters that are not of national interest. Federal influence on public education through grant monies and special education laws are currently debated.
Fourteenth Amendment guarantees that persons cannot be deprived of life, liberty, or property by the states without due process of law.	The incorporation of the due process clause to the states through landmark Supreme Court cases has shifted power to the federal government. Examples: *Engel v. Vitale*; *Tinker v. Des Moines*; *Gideon v. Wainwright*; *Roe v. Wade*; and *McDonald v. Chicago*.
Commerce Clause provides Congress the power to regulate commerce with foreign nations and among the states.	Originally, the clause applied to the movement of goods and trade from state to state. Now, almost every activity is considered interstate commerce and federal government can regulate it. During the Civil Rights movement, Congress used the clause to end discrimination in private businesses. However, *U.S. v. Lopez* (1995) limited Congress' use of the commerce clause when applied to public schools.
Necessary and Proper Clause provides Congress implied powers to carry out the 17 expressed powers written in the Constitution.	This clause, also called the "elastic clause," is an enlargement of the powers expressly granted to Congress. As evidenced in the *McCulloch* case, the clause upheld the creation of a central bank.

2. The balance of power between the national and states governments has changed over time based on U.S. Supreme Court interpretation of such cases as:

- *McCulloch v Maryland* (1819), which declared that Congress has implied powers necessary to implement its enumerated powers and established supremacy of the U.S. Constitution and federal laws over state laws.

- *United States v Lopez* (1995), which ruled that Congress may not use the commerce clause to make possession of a gun in a school zone a federal crime, introducing a new phase of federalism that recognized the importance of state sovereignty and local control.

McCulloch v. Maryland (1819)

Constitutional Issue: Necessary and Proper Clause; Supremacy Clause

Questions: Does Congress have the constitutional power to create a nation bank?
Does a state have the constitutional power to tax a national bank chartered by Congress?

Background
In 1816, Congress created the Second Bank of the United States, which opened a branch in Baltimore. In 1818, the Maryland legislature passed an act that taxes out-of-state banks operating in the state. The law specifically targeted the Bank of the United States, since it was the only such back operating in the state. The head cashier, James McCulloch, refused to pay the state tax, claiming Maryland's government did not have the right to tax a national bank. Maryland's leaders sued, and the state courts upheld the tax law. The bank's lawyers appealed the case to the Supreme Court.

Holding and Reasoning
The U.S. Constitution and national laws are supreme over state laws. Congress has the authority to expand its expressed powers through the necessary and proper clause.

The Supreme Court held in a 7-0 ruling that Congress has implied constitutional powers to create a national bank and that individual states could not tax a federally chartered bank. The majority opinion stated that the Constitution, by nature, must be general in order to adapt to unforeseen circumstances. Therefore, Congress must have some implied powers to allow it to exercise the broad range of expressed powers given it in Article I, Section 8 of the Constitution. The language "necessary and proper" should be construed to mean "convenient, or useful, or essential" and that language is purposely included among the powers of Congress, not the limitations, and so should be read as enlarging the scope of Congress' powers.

As to whether Maryland could tax the federal bank, the power to tax something is the power to destroy it. Since the states are necessarily inferior to the federal government, the states do not have the power to "destroy" (by taxing) the federal government. The people did not design to make their federal government dependent on the states. The Supremacy Clause of the United States Constitution (Article VI, Clause 2) establishes that the Constitution, federal laws, and treaties made under its authority, constitute the supreme law of the land.

U.S. v. Lopez (1995)

Constitutional Issue: Commerce clause, Article I, Section 8 (Powers of Congress); Due Process clause of the Fourteenth Amendment.

Question: Is the 1990 Gun-Free School Zones Act, forbidding individuals from knowingly carrying a gun in a school zone, unconstitutional because it exceeds the power of Congress to legislate under the Commerce Clause?

Background

In 1992 Alfonso Lopez, Jr., a 12th-grade student in San Antonio, Texas, took a concealed .38-calibre handgun and five bullets into his high school. The gun was loaded and Lopez had five backup rounds of ammunition tucked away in his jeans. School officials confronted Lopez, and he admitted that he had a gun. Lopez was charged with violating the Gun-Free School Zones Act, which made it unlawful for a person to possess a firearm in a school zone. The maximum penalty was five years of imprisonment. Lopez entered a plea of not guilty, and his attorneys moved to dismiss the charge on the grounds that Congress was not allowed to create laws that essentially control public school districts. The U.S. government argued that possession of the gun in a school zone could result in a violent crime that would have the potential to have an impact on the national economy. The government also claimed that the significant cost of insurance associated with violent crime affects the economy, because the expense is spread throughout society.

Holding and Reasoning

Congress may not use the commerce clause to make possession of a gun in a school zone a federal crime.

In a 5-4 decision, the Supreme Court rejected the government's claim, holding that the law was not substantially related to commerce. The majority opinion held, "Under the theories that the Government presents...it is difficult to perceive any limitation on federal power, even in areas...where States historically have been sovereign. Thus, if we were to accept the Government's arguments, we are hard-pressed to posit any activity by an individual that Congress is without power to regulate...." The Supreme Court also cited the Founders' speeches and writings on the balance between state and federal power, and in particular their belief in limited government: the federal government did not have any powers except those delegated to it in the Constitution. *U.S. v. Lopez* is a particularly significant case because it marked the first time in half a century that the Court held Congress had overstepped its power under the Commerce Clause.

C. Explain how the distribution of powers among the three federal branches and between national and state governments impacts policy making.

1. Multiple access points for stakeholders and institutions to influence public policy flows from the allocation of powers between national and state governments.

2. National policymaking is constrained by the sharing power between and among the three branches and state governments.

   Commentary: Policy making requires agreement among the three branches of the federal government and frequently cooperation by the states. For example, immigration law passed by Congress and signed by the President must be enforced by the Executive Branch through the Department of Homeland Security and Immigration and Custom Enforcement (ICE). The Supreme Court usually limits their interpretation on immigration law but recently upheld President Trump's executive order to limit persons immigrating from six Muslim countries in the name of national security. States and cities that claim "sanctuary status" and protect foreign nationals who enter without permission, face legal challenges by a Congress and Executive Branch that clearly have constitutional authority on this issue. Multiple access points for citizens to enter the debate (Congress, states, relief organizations) have made the immigration issue contentious and call into question state actions that conflict with federal law.

Practice Multiple Choice

"These two clauses have been the sources of much virulent invective and petulant declamation against the proposed constitution, they have been held up to the people, in all the exaggerated colors of misrepresentation, as the pernicious engines by which their local governments were to be destroyed and their liberties exterminated — as the hideous monster whose devouring jaws would spare neither sex nor age, nor high nor low, nor sacred nor profane; and yet strange as it may appear, after all this clamor, to those who may not have happened to contemplate them in the same light, it may be affirmed with perfect confidence, that the constitutional operation of the intended government would be precisely the same, if these clauses were entirely obliterated, as if they were repeated in every article."

Alexander Hamilton, *The Federalist* paper number 33

1. Which of the following statements best summarizes Hamilton's argument?

   A. The powers given the federal government by the Constitution will not destroy representative democracy.
   B. The Constitution lacks clauses that protect individual liberties
   C. The powers of the federal government should be balanced with the sovereignty of the states.
   D. The Constitution will not substantially change the powers of the national government when compared to the Articles of Confederation.

2. Which of the following constitutional clauses does Hamilton refer to in this essay?

   A. Judicial review and supremacy clause
   B. Necessary and proper and commerce
   C. Enumerated powers and executive privilege
   D. Equal protection and due process

3. According to Hamilton, why are these two clauses not cause for concern?

    A. The Constitution prohibits the government from restricting individual liberties.
    B. The people can easily amend the Constitution to limit government power.
    C. State governments will continue to have power over their citizens.
    D. The opponents of the Constitution are outnumbered and will be defeated during the ratification process.

4. Since the ratification of the Constitution, how has the federal government used its power to limit the influence of state and local governments?

    A. By awarding block grants and aid to the states.
    B. By conducting all national elections.
    C. By establishing national marriage and divorce laws.
    D. By ending racial discrimination public school and private businesses.

Answers: A, B, C, D

Practice Multiple Choice

SANCTUARY CITIES AND STATES, 2018

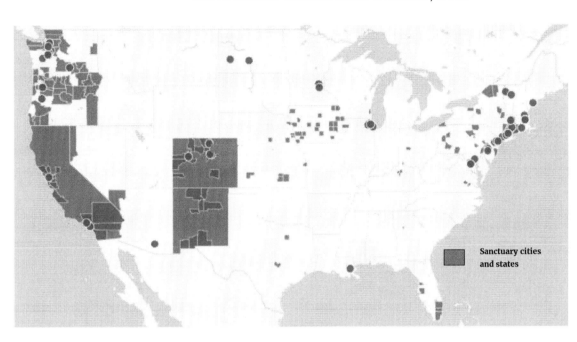

Source: Chicago Tribune, 2008.

Note: Sanctuary status generally refers to a city or other jurisdiction that asks its local authorities to not check the federal status of immigrants

1. Which of the following statements best decribes the pattern illustrated on the map?

    A. Sanctuary cities are predominantly located along the coasts of the United States.
    B. Immigation of undocumented workers is a problem primarily laong the southern border.
    C. California provides more social welfare benefits to new immigrants than any other state.
    D. The southern states do not have an issue with the migration of immigrants from Mexico.

2. What does the data imply about political ideology in the United States?

    A. Undocumented immigrants are protected by a strong conservative ideology in the western U.S.

    B. The decision to offer sanctuary status does not separate the nation based on political ideology.

    C. The libertarian movement has prevented the spread of sanctuary status across the United States.

    D. The nation is divided on the issue of treatment of undocumented immigrants with centers of liberal ideology in favor of sanctuary status.

Answers: A, D,

Practice Multiple Choice

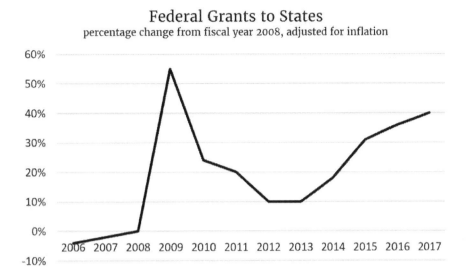

1. Which of the following is an accurate statement about the information in the line graph?
   A. Federal grants to the states has remained fairly constant when takeing inflation into account.
   B. The amount of federal grants to the states has fluctuated greatly between 2008 and 2017.
   C. In general, states do not rely much on federal funds to operate their programs.
   D. States requested fewer grants in 2012 and 2013 than in 2016 and 2017.

2. Based on the information in the line graph, which of the following is the most likely explanation of the change in federal grants to states in 2009.
   A. Barack Obama was elected president and decided to decentralize government by transferring budget money to the states.
   B. Conservatives came to power and awarded new military contracts to defense industries.
   C. The economy collapsed and the federal government reacted by boosting aid to the states.
   D. States decreased taxation and needed a new source of funds to offset lower revenue.

Answers: B, C

Practice Free Response Question: Type 1 – Concept Application

President **Donald Trump**'s ... threat to strip federal grant money from sanctuary cities sets up a battle between the new president and more than 300 cities, counties, states and institutions that could play out in the courts and Congress.... A sanctuary generally refers to a city or other jurisdiction that asks its local authorities to not check the federal status of immigrants. What the president ... and what the sanctuary areas themselves will do is not yet clear, but the actions do fulfill a pledge that animated Trump's campaign and advances a struggle between Trump and the sanctuary areas that emerged over the months leading up to the election. Chicago has been a sanctuary city since 1985, and Mayor **Rahm Emanuel** has spoken out strongly about maintaining that status.

Chicago Tribune, January 26, 2017

After reading the scenario, respond to A, B, and C below.

A. Describe a power the President can use to fulfill his threat described in the scenario.

B. In the context of the scenario, explain how the president's action can be affected by interaction with Congress.

C. In the context of the scenario, explain how the battle between President and states will be affected by provisions in the U.S. Constitution.

Exemplary Answer

A. *The President can* file lawsuits against the sanctuary-observing cities, counties and states for violating federal law. He can also issue an executive order and withhold federal grant money for local law enforcement agencies.

B. Congress may disagree with the President's decision to cut off grant money to states and cities and pass legislation that requires the government to provide funding without condition.

C. The supremacy clause of the U.S. Constitution means that when federal and state laws conflict, the national government has the power to determine the policy. Immigration is a federal power, not a state power reserved by the Tenth Amendment, so the federal laws would trump.

Practice Free Response Question: Type 3 – Supreme Court Comparison

Directions: Respond to each part of the question below and separate your answers using the A, B, and C indicators. This FRQ is worth four points based on the breakdown below. You have 20-minutes to complete your answer.

- Part A: identify the similarity between the court cases
- Part B1: provide factual information about *McCulloch v. Maryland*
- Part B2: explain how that information is relevant to *United States v. Comstock* (2010)
- Part C: describe an interaction between *United States v Comstock* (2010) and Congress.

Six days before Graydon Earl Comstock was to have completed a 37-month sentence for receiving child pornography, the U.S. Attorney General certified that Comstock was a sexually dangerous person. The Attorney General was applying the Adam Walsh Child Protection Safety Act which allows the government to continue to detain prisoners who had engaged in sexually violent conduct, suffered from mental illness and would have difficulty controlling themselves. If the government is able to prove all of this to a judge by "clear and convincing" evidence, it may hold such prisoners until they are no longer dangerous or a state assumes responsibility for them. Lower courts had previously found the provision to hold an offender past completion of their sentence was unconstitutional. Comstock argued that Congress did not possess the authority to hold "sexually dangerous" inmates indefinitely.

In the ensuing case, *United States v. Comstock* (2010), the Supreme Court held in a 7-2 decision that the Constitution grants Congress the authority to extend the federal prison sentences of dangerous sex offenders. The majority decision stated that Congress has the expressed power to create a prison system and to punish people who violate criminal laws, though neither power is explicitly mentioned in the Constitution.

A. Identify the constitutional clause that is common to both *United States v. Comstock* (2010) and *McCulloch v. Maryland* (1819).

B. Based on the constitutional clause identified in part A, explain why the facts of *McCulloch v. Maryland* (1819) led to a similar holding in *United States v. Comstock* (2010).

C. Describe an action Congress may take to ensure that similar sex offenders are treated equally under the law.

Exemplary Answer

A. *The constitutional clause in common to both the Comstock and McCullouch cases is the "necessary and proper" clause which allows Congress implied powers to carry out their expressed powers in the Constitution.*

B. *In the McCullouch case, the Supreme Court, for the first time interpreted the necessary and proper clause to allow Congress to extend their powers to borrow money by creating a national bank. In the Comstock holding, the court determined it was necessary and proper for Congress to extended a prison sentence since it had the expressed power to determine punishments for federal crimes.*

C. *One way that Congress can ensure that sex offenders' sentences are treated equally is to amend the Adam Walsh Child Protection Act to set specific guidelines on "clear and convincing" evidence and on the length of extensions to sentences.*

Practice Free Response Question: Type 3 –Supreme Court Comparison

Directions: Respond to each part of the question below and separate your answers using the A, B, and C indicators. This FRQ is worth four points based on the breakdown below. You have 20-minutes to complete your answer.

- Part A: identify the similarity between the court cases
- Part B: provide factual information about *U.S. v. Lopez* (1995).
- Part B: explain how that information is relevant to *Gonzales v. Raich* (2005).
- Part C: describe an interaction between *Gonzales v. Raich* (2005).and Congress.

In 1970, Congress passed the Controlled Substances Act (CSA) which categorized illegal drugs into different "schedules" and prevented their sale, purchase, and possession in the United States. In 1996, California enacted the Compassionate Use Act that allowed the use of medical marijuana within the state by persons needing it for legitimate medical purposes. Angel Raich and Diane Monson were California residents who both legally used marijuana to treat legitimate medical issues. Despite receiving approval from California state officials, federal agents seized and destroyed Raich's marijuana plants. Raich brought suit against Alberto Gonzales, Attorney General of the United States, prohibiting the enforcement of the federal CSA.

In a 6-3 decision, the Supreme Court held that Congress has the power to regulate the use of home-grown marijuana in a state where consumption for medical purposes is legal because in aggregate the activity could have a substantial effect on a national marijuana market.

A. Identify the constitutional clause that is common to both *Gonzales v. Raich* (2005) and *U.S. v. Lopez* (1995).

B. Based on the constitutional clause identified in part A, explain why the facts of *U.S. v. Lopez* (1995) led to a different holding than the holding of *Gonzales v. Raich* (2005).

C. Describe another action that the U.S. Congress could take to uphold the court's decision in *Gonzales v. Raich* (2005).

Exemplary Answer

A. *The constitutional clause in common to both the* Raich *and* Lopez *cases is the interstate commerce clause which allows Congress to regulate transactions that occur across state lines.*

B. *In* U.S. v. Lopez, *the courts held that the interstate commerce clause did not apply to public schools. The purchase of the gun did not involve national commerce and the public schools are the responsibility of the states. In* Raich, *the marijuana to supply Americans with a medical use would affect a national market and therefore Congress could regulate its trade.*

C. *One way Congress could support the court's decision upholding regulation of marijuana sales is by passing strict criminal laws on production or by passing a high tax on production or sales. Congress could justify its actions by showing the costs to the public (injuries, deaths, and ER services).*

Practice Free Response Question: Type 4 –Argumentative Essay

Develop an argument that explains how the Founders created a competitive policy-making process to ensure the people's will is represented.

In your essay, you must:
- Present a defensible thesis that responds to the prompt and establishes a line of reasoning.
- Support your thesis with at least TWO pieces of accurate and relevant information:
  - At least ONE piece of evidence must be from one of the following foundational documents:
    - Federalist No. 51
    - Federalist No. 10
    - U.S. Constitution
  - Use a second piece of evidence from another foundational document from the list or from your study of the policy making process
- Use reasoning to explain why your evidence supports your thesis
- Respond to an opposing or alternative perspective using refutation, concession, or rebuttal

Exemplary Answer

The Founders created a national government based on the Madisonian model of republicanism, separation of powers, and federalism to ensure that policy-making reflected the people's will and not an elitist faction. **[Thesis]**

In Federalist 51, James Madison describes how a large society divided among many factions would have to work together through a national Congress to achieve major decisions. Factions would be able to control areas of the nation, perhaps even states, but designing a competition between regions that had specialized economies and different living patterns would ensure democracy. **[Relevant evidence 1; supports thesis]** *Previously, the colonists had experienced an elitist British Parliament of nobles that had passed punitive acts against them. The creation of a Congress with a House directly elected by the people and a Senate chosen by leaders of the separate states would ensure competition between factions. Only strong common agreement among different factions, the people's choice, would become national law.* **[Reasoning]**

The Constitution respects that the will of the people is best decided at the state and local level. Amendment 10 reserves all rights not given the national government (or prohibited the states) to the states and people. States enjoy the power to design their own public education systems, create cities, and promote business. The people's will is not standard across the U.S. and neither are the cultures and laws and priorities of the states. The Founders recognized and promoted diversity in a large republic. **[Relevant evidence 2]**

Although the structure of our government invites competition, the politics of our system has been controlled by a two-party system. Making policy requires majority votes, and since the inception of the Constitution, the wealthy and educated of every era have had the resources and organization to create national parties. These parties raise money to fund candidates that support a narrow ideology. And policymaking usually reflects one dominant ideology at any given time in U.S. history. **[Alternative Perspective]**

UNIT 2: INTERACTION AMONG BRANCHES OF GOVERNMENT

Enduring Understanding CONSTITUTIONALISM-3: The republican ideas in the U.S. is manifested in the structure and operation of the legislative branch.

A. Describe the different structures, powers, and function of each house of Congress.

1. The Senate is designed to represent states equally, while the House is designed to represent the population.

2. Different chamber sizes and constituents influence formality of debate.

3. Coalitions in Congress are affected by term-length differences.

Commentary: A **congressional caucus** is a group of members of the U.S. Congress that meets to pursue common legislative objectives. In addition to the term caucus, they are sometimes called conferences, coalitions, or working groups. Some caucuses are organized political factions with a common ideological orientation. Examples include:

- The Tuesday Morning Caucus is a group of approximately 40 center-right Republicans dedicated to promoting fiscal responsibility, personal independence and a strong national defense.
- The House Freedom Caucus was established in 2015. Its approximately 35 conservative members promote what it considers limited government, the rule of law, liberty, safety, and prosperity.
- The Congressional Black Caucus was founded in 1971 as an advocacy group seeking equality for Black Americans, especially in under-served communities.
- Congressional Progressive Caucus, founded in 1991 based on concern about the economic hardships of economic recession and the growing inequality brought about by a weak Democratic Party response to the Republican majority in the House of Representatives.

Comparing the House and Senate

	House of Representatives	Senate
Terms	Two years	Six years
Membership	435	100
Elections	All every two years	One-third every two years
Constituents	Congressional districts	States
Unique Powers	• Initiates all spending bills through the House Ways and Means Committee • Brings impeachment charges	• Advise and consent to approve treaties by two-thirds vote • Confirm judicial and executive appointments • Try impeachment charges (removal power)
Differences in Operation	• More centralized, more formal • Rules Committee very powerful in controlling the time and rules of debate with strong influence by the Speaker of the House) • Emphasizes tax and revenue policy • Power in centralized in the Speaker's inner circle of advisors (Majority leader, whips and committee chairs) • 20 standing and select committees; members are policy specialists and each serve on about 5 committees • Turnover is higher than the Senate, although incumbents almost always win re-election	• Less centralized, less formal • No rules committee; limits of debate come through unanimous consent or cloture or filibuster • Emphasis on foreign policy • Larger personal staffs • 20 standing and select committees; members are policy generalists, with each member on about 7 committees • Turnover rate is minimal

4. The enumerated and implied powers in the Constitution allow the creation of public policy by Congress, which includes:

Enumerated Power (Article I, Section 8)	Implied Powers Based on Necessary and Proper clause, Article I, Section 8, clause 18
To collect taxes for the general welfare of the United States	• To create the Internal Revenue Service (IRS) to collect taxes • To spend revenue on roads, housing, medical care, education, etc.
To raise and support armies and a navy	• To create a draft (selective service requirement) • To create an Air Force • To create the interstate highway system (for national defense)
To regulate commerce	• To prohibit job discrimination based on race, gender, or age • To break up monopolies • To set health standards (regulations) for food • To pass minimum wage laws
To borrow money and to coin money and regulate its value	• To create a national bank (Bank of the U.S.; Federal Reserve)

B. Explain how the structures, powers, and functions of both houses of Congress affect the policy-making process.

1. By design, the different structures, powers, and functions of the U.S. Senate and House of Representatives affect the policy-making process.

2. Though both chambers rely on committees to conduct hearings and debate bills under consideration, different constitutional responsibilities of the House and Senate affect the policy-making process.

3. Chamber-specific procedures, rules, and roles that impact the policy-making process include:
   - **The filibuster**: Senate rules permit a Senator, or a series of Senators, to speak for as long as they wish, and on any topic they choose, unless three-fifths of the Senators bring the debate to a close by invoking cloture. In 2013, the Senate used the so-called "nuclear option" to eliminate the use of the filibuster on executive branch nominees and judicial nominees, *except* to the Supreme Court. On April 6, 2017, the Senate eliminated the sole remaining exception to the 2013 change by invoking the "nuclear option" for Supreme Court nominees.

- **Roles of Speaker of the House, President of the Senate, party leadership, and committee leadership in both chambers.**

Role	Influence
Speaker of the House: is the top leadership position of the majority party; he/she actively works to set that party's legislative agenda; elected by members of the majority party.	• Determines priority of bills and refers them to committees • Appoints House members to standing and conference committees • Signs all bills and resolutions passed by House
President of the Senate: Senate's presiding officer, equivalent to the Speaker of the House of Representatives, but powers are more limited	• Manages and schedules the legislative and executive business of the Senate • Appoints committee chairs and members • Refers bills to committees
Senate Majority Leader: effectively the most powerful position in the Senate; elected by members of the majority party in the Senate.	• Lead speaker for the majority party during floor debates • Develops the calendar • Assists the president and speaker with program development, policy formation and policy decisions
Majority and Minority Whips: Congressmen who assist the Speaker and Majority Leader in acquiring votes.	• Ensure member attendance • Ensure a majority of votes are secure before putting legislation on the floor
Committee Chairmen: appointed leaders of the Senate and House permanent standing committees.	• Sets committee's agenda, determining when or if bills will be considered. • Calls, presides, and maintains order over meetings.

- **Holds:** An informal practice when a senator informs the floor leader that he/she does not wish a particular bill to reach the floor for consideration, signaling a potential filibuster.

- **Unanimous consent:** A senator may request to set aside a specified rule of procedure in order to quicken proceedings. Example: a request to limit time on debate.

- **Role of the Rules Committee**: considers all bills reported from House standing committees and determines whether, and in what order, to schedule their consideration on the floor of the House.

- **Role of the Committee of the Whole**: the entire House of Representatives sits as a committee and operates under informal parliamentary rules. Example: When the House receives the President for the State of the Union address or a foreign dignitary.

- **Discharge petitions in the House**: bring bills out of committee and to the House floor for consideration without a report from the committee by "discharging" the committee from further consideration of a bill or resolution. The discharge petition allows a majority of the House of Representatives to force a floor vote on a bill, even if the leadership, who usually controls what legislation makes it to the floor, is opposed.

- **Treaty ratification and confirmation role in the Senate**: the two most common and effective ways to check the power of the executive branch. The Senate confirms appointments of top executive officials by majority vote and ratifies treaties by the advice and consent of a two-thirds vote.

| Most powerful standing committees ||
House	Senate
Ways and Means Committee: According to the Constitution, all revenue bills (Tax, import duties) must originate here.	**Foreign Relations:** determines the budget and confirms appointments of State Department; approves foreign aid and arms sales.
Rules Committee: Most powerful committee, serves as "traffic cop" in House, directing flow of all legislation. Can hold bills back or stop them completely.	**Finance:** considers all bills related to revenue, including tariffs, Medicare, and Medicaid.
Appropriations Committee: Most expenditures are first approved by this committee; has power to influence an agency's policies by "marking up" an agency's budget	**Appropriations Committee:** Most expenditures are first approved by this committee; has power to influence an agency's policies by "marking up" an agency's budget

4. Congress must generate a budget that addressed both discretionary and mandatory spending, and as entitlement costs grow, discretionary spending opportunities will decrease unless tax revenues increase or the budget deficit increases.

Commentary: Discretionary spending occurs when Congress appropriates annual bills to fund programs such as defense, education, and transportation. Funding for these programs vary according to national and political priorities. These funds are subject to enforcement rules that differ from those that apply to mandatory spending. **Mandatory spending** includes funds for **entitlement programs** and certain other payments to people, businesses, and state and local governments. Mandatory spending is generally determined by law-binding, ongoing commitments to citizens. The laws set eligibility requirements and benefit rules. The three largest entitlement programs are Social Security, Medicare, and Medicaid. Unemployment compensation, retirement programs for federal employees, student loans, and deposit insurance are also mandatory expenditures. Approximately 60 percent of federal spending is mandatory.

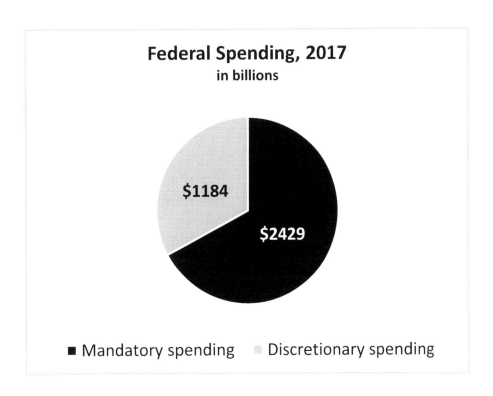

Federal Spending, 2017
in billions

$1184

$2429

■ Mandatory spending   Discretionary spending

Mandatory Spending, Fiscal Year 2017

Program	Spending (in billions)	% of mandatory spending
Social Security, Unemployment, and Labor	$1,360	48
Medicare and Health	$1,120	39
Food and Agriculture	$126	4
Veterans' Benefits	$104	4
Transportation	$84	3
Housing and Community	$22	1
Education	$12	<1
Energy and Environment	$10	<1
Military	$10	<1
International Affairs	$4	<1
Science	$ 1	<1
TOTAL	$2800	

Source: Office of Management and Budget, 2017

Discretionary Spending, Fiscal Year 2017

Program	Spending (in billions)	% of discretionary spending
Military	$622.6	54
Veterans' Benefits	$75.4	7
Education	$72.8	6
Government	$69	6
Housing and Community	$68.5	6
Medicare and Health	$58.6	5
International Affairs	$41.4	4
Energy and Environment	$41.3	4
Social Security, Unemployment, and Labor	$31.7	3
Science	$30.7	3
Transportation	$24.7	2
Food and Agriculture	$12.8	1
TOTAL	$1150	

Source: Office of Management and Budget, 2017

5. Pork barrel legislation and logrolling affect lawmaking in both chambers.
   - **Pork barrel legislation**: refers to spending on federal projects, grants, and contracts for cities, businesses, colleges, and institutions that will win the votes of key legislators and allow them to claim credit for helping their constituents during re-election. Pork has led to the passage of large omnibus bills, thousands of pages in length that are not read by Congress before voting. The volume of legislation serves to hide the pork provisions that are specific handouts to members of Congress and their constituents.

   - **Logrolling:** legislators support a bill sponsored by another Congressman in return for support of his or her bill.

C. Explain how congressional behavior is influenced by election processes, partisanship, and divided government.

   1. Congressional behavior and governing effectiveness are influenced by:
      - Ideological divisions within Congress that can lead to gridlock or create the need for negotiations and compromise.

      - Gerrymandering, redistricting, and unequal representation of constituencies have been partially addressed in such Court decisions such as *Baker v. Carr* (1961), which opened the door to equal protection challenges to redistricting and stated the "one-person, one vote" doctrine, and the no-racial gerrymandering decision of *Shaw v Reno* (1993).

      Gerrymandering occurs when the drawing of legislative district boundaries benefits a party, group, or incumbent.

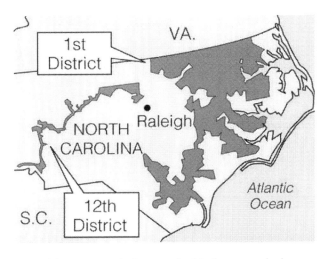

Shaw v Reno (1993)

Constitutional Issue: Equal Protection Clause, Fourteenth Amendment

Question: Did North Carolina's racially gerrymandered district violate the Fourteenth Amendment's Equal Protection Clause?

Background

North Carolina submitted to the Department of Justice a map with one majority-minority black district—that is, a district with a black majority. The Department of Justice believed that the state could have drawn another such majority-minority district in order to improve representation of black voters rather than including them all within one district. The state revised its map and submitted a new plan, this one with two majority-minority districts. The proposed 12th district was 160 miles (260 km) long, winding through the state to connect various areas having in common only a large black population. The plan was challenged by white voters (Shaw) who claimed that the plan was racially discriminatory, its only purpose being to elect a black representative. The case reached the Supreme Court after being rejected by the district court.

Holding and Reasoning

Legislative redistricting must be conscience of race and ensure compliance with the Voting Rights Act of 1965.

The Court held that although North Carolina's reapportionment plan was racially neutral on its face, the resulting district shape was bizarre enough to suggest that it constituted an effort to separate voters into different districts based on race. The unusual district seemed to exceed what was reasonably necessary to avoid racial imbalances. The Court ruled that the plaintiffs did present a valid equal protection challenge that must be examined under strict scrutiny. As such, efforts to satisfy §5 or §2 of the Voting Rights Act must be narrowly tailored to those purposes and does not give the government free reign to gerrymander districts based solely on race. Legislative and congressional districts will be struck down by courts for violating the Equal Protection Clause if they cannot be explained on grounds other than race. "Bizarrely shaped" districts are strongly indicative of racial intent.

Baker v Carr (1961)

Constitutional Issue: Equal Protection Clause, Fourteenth Amendment

Question: Does the Supreme Court have jurisdiction to hear cases involving the drawing of legislative districts (reapportionment)?

Background

Charles Baker, the mayor of Nashville, filed suit in federal court against Joe C. Carr, the Tennessee Secretary of State to challenge the apportionment of state legislators in the state of Tennessee. While the state constitution required that legislative districts be redrawn every ten years according to the federal census, the redistricts had not been redrawn since 1901. Since that time, urban areas had grown vastly in population and were subsequently underrepresented. They sought to have the apportionment law declared unconstitutional and to obtain an injunction restraining the conduct of further elections under the law. Baker also requested the court to order an election at large for members of the state legislature or to order an election with equitably apportioned legislative districts based on the most recent census figures. The federal district court refused to hear the case arguing that they did not have jurisdiction to hear cases involving the drawing of legislative districts because this was a "political question" to be answered by the elected branches of government.

Holding and Reasoning

Under the equal protection clause of the Fourteenth Amendment, federal courts have jurisdiction to hear cases involving reapportionment.

In a 6-2 decision, the Supreme Court ruled in favor of Baker. The Court ultimately concluded that "the complaint's allegations of a denial of equal protection ... are entitled to a trial and a decision." Thus, the Supreme Court gained power to rule on apportionment laws. Each person's vote became protected under the 14th amendment and the "one person, one vote" policy. Biased reapportionment was totally done away with and changed the fundamental voting structure of the United States. A balance of power shifted to urban centers from rural areas in states like Tennessee.

Since the earliest days of the republic, redrawing the boundaries of congressional districts after each census has been primarily the responsibility of state legislatures. Following World War I, as the nation's population began to shift from rural to urban areas, many legislatures lost their enthusiasm for the task and failed to carry out their constitutional responsibility.

Redistricting (or reapportionment) refers to the process of states redrawing congressional districts every 10 years on the basis of the census. Redistricting accommodates population shifts and keep districts as equal as possible in population.

Malapportionment refers to an unequal or unfair distribution of representatives to a legislative body.

- The effectiveness of Congress is also influenced by elections that have led to a divided government, including partisan votes against presidential initiatives and congressional refusal to confirm appointments of "lame-duck" presidents of the opposite party.

- Congressional effectiveness is also determined by different role conceptions of "trustee," "delegate," and "politico" as related to constituent accountability in each chamber.

  Trustee refers to a role played by elected representatives who listen to constituents' opinions and then use their best judgment to make final decisions.

  Delegate refers to a role played by elected representatives who vote the way their constituents would want them to, regardless of their own opinions.

  Politico refers to a role played by elected representatives who act as trustees or as delegates, depending on the issue.

Enduring Understanding: The presidency has been enhanced beyond its expressed constitutional powers.

A. Explain how the president can implement a policy agenda.
  1. Presidents use powers and perform functions of the office to accomplish a policy agenda.

     Commentary: The President exercises more power than the Constitution suggests. Since the Great Depression and World War II, the president dominates the congressional agenda, and the term chief legislator is frequently used to emphasize his pre-eminence in the legislative process. Presidents believe the public elected them to implement a mandate – their campaign promises. And Congress should be willing partners to pass his agenda. The threat of a presidential veto is enough for Congress to allow the President to initiate legislation that he will sign. Approximately 4% of all vetoed bills have been overridden by Congress since the nation's founding. Although the President cannot formally introduce a bill to Congress, members of the president's party collaborate to create legislation favorable to the president's agenda and usher it through the legislative process.

2. Formal and informal powers of the president include:

- **Vetoes** - formal powers that enable the president to check Congress. A veto refers to a presidential rejection of a bill.

- **Pocket vetoes** –If Congress adjourns within 10 days after submitting a bill, the president can simply let it die by neither signing nor vetoing it.

- **Foreign policy** –The Constitution allocates certain formal powers in the realm of national security that are exclusive to the executive. For example, the president is **Commander-in-Chief** of the country's armed forces – he is supreme commander of the military forces of the U.S. and of the state National Guard units when they are called into federal service. The president has the sole power to **negotiate treaties** with other nations, subject to the agreement of two-thirds of the Senate. Informal powers include presidential negotiations of **executive agreements** with the heads of foreign governments; unlike treaties, executive agreements do not require Senate ratification; only a majority vote of Congress is needed. U.S. trade agreements such as the North American Free Trade Agreement (NAFTA), World Trade Organization agreements, and bilateral free trade agreements (FTAs) have been approved by majority vote of each house rather than by two-thirds vote of the Senate.

- **Bargaining and persuasion** – Bargaining – trading support on policies or providing specific benefits for representatives and senators is not a common strategy used by presidents. The greatest leverage of presidential power occurs in the first year of his term, referred to as the "honeymoon" period when the Congress accepts the President's priorities as a mandate from voters.

- Once a bill becomes law, the president can make his interpretation of the law clear to Congress and the public by issuing a **signing statement**.

- **Executive Orders:** are formal methods where the president can direct an agency by issuing an executive order outlining a certain way to do things. Famous Executive Orders include Lincoln's Emancipation Proclamation; FDR's internment of Japanese-Americans during World War II; Truman's Desegregation of the Armed Forces.

B. Explain how the president's agenda can create tension and frequent confrontations with Congress.

1. The potential for conflict with the Senate depends upon the type of executive branch appointments, including:

    Commentary: One of the president's most important roles is presiding over the administration of government. The Constitution charges the president with faithfully executing the law. Today, the federal bureaucracy includes more than four million civilian and military employees and spends more than $3 trillion annually. One of the greatest powers of a U.S. President is the ability to appoint top-level administrators. New presidents can appoint approximately 3,000 cabinet and subcabinet officers and agency executives. The appointments assessed on the AP exam include:

    - **Cabinet members** refer to the group of presidential advisors including 14 secretaries and the attorney general. Each member of the cabinet heads an executive department of thousands of federal employees and multi-million and multi-billion-dollar budgets.

    - **Ambassadors:** In addition, presidents appoint diplomats to represent the U.S. in other countries. They represent the President in an official capacity and are charged with protecting and promoting national interests, organizing visits, welcoming visitors, and supporting resolutions.

    - **White House staff:** includes aides the president sees daily – the chief of staff, congressional liaison aides, the press secretary, and national security advisor. Presidents rely heavily on their staffs for information. The Executive Office of the President is housed at the White House and includes three major policymaking bodies: the **National Security Council** (to help the president coordinate foreign and defense policy), the **Council of Economic Advisers,** and the **Office of Management and Budget** (to create an annual budget and oversee the spending of all federal government departments and agencies).

2. Senate confirmation is an important check on appointment powers, but the president's longest lasting influence lies in the life-tenured judicial appointments.

3. Policy initiatives and executive orders promoted by the president often lead to conflict with the congressional agenda.

C. Explain how presidents have interpreted and justified their use of formal and informal powers.

1. Justification for a single executive are set forth in **Federalist No. 70**.

Commentary: Alexander Hamilton's Federalist No. 70 is one of the most referenced essays concerning the presidency. Hamilton writes, "energy in the executive" is one of the most important parts of the executive department of the country, as defined in the Constitution. This "energy" is one of the most written about components and excuses for expansion of presidential power, especially in the 20th century. The office of the president was purposely created to provide the authority, secrecy, and swiftness necessary to govern a large and growing republic and most importantly for Hamilton, to protect private property. The Hamiltonian model of government (a strong executive who protects private property) is a clear contrast to the Madisonian model (a divided government instituted to protect individual liberties from majority faction).

Main Ideas of Federalist 70 and Critical Passages
• **The executive branch should be composed of a unitary executive (not a council) with powers independent of Congress.**
"…all men of sense will agree in the necessity of an energetic Executive, it will only remain to inquire, what are the ingredients which constitute this energy?… The ingredients which constitute energy in the Executive are, first, unity; secondly, duration; thirdly, an adequate provision for its support; fourthly, competent powers…. This unity may be destroyed in two ways: either by vesting the power in two or more magistrates of equal dignity and authority; or by vesting it ostensibly in one man, subject, in whole or in part, to the control and co-operation of others, in the capacity of counsellors to him…. Wherever two or more persons are engaged in any common enterprise or pursuit, there is always danger of difference of opinion. If it be a public trust or office, in which they are clothed with equal dignity and authority, there is peculiar danger of personal emulation and even animosity…. And what is still worse, they might split the community into the most violent and irreconcilable factions, adhering differently to the different individuals who composed the magistracy."

Main Ideas of Federalist 70 and Critical Passages
• **A single executive directly accountable to the people will best secure the safety of the republic.** "Taking it for granted that all men of sense will agree in the necessity of an energetic Executive, it will only remain to inquire ... [h]ow far can they be combined with those other ingredients which constitute safety in the republican sense?... The ingredients which constitute safety in the republican sense are, first, a due dependence on the people, secondly, a due responsibility.... But one of the weightiest objections to a plurality in the Executive, and which lies as much against the last as the first plan, is, that it tends to conceal faults and destroy responsibility. Responsibility is of two kinds — to censure and to punishment. The first is the more important of the two, especially in an elective office. Man, in public trust, will much oftener act in such a manner as to render him unworthy of being any longer trusted, than in such a manner as to make him obnoxious to legal punishment. But the multiplication of the Executive adds to the difficulty of detection in either case. It often becomes impossible, amidst mutual accusations, to determine on whom the blame or the punishment of a pernicious measure, or series of pernicious measures, ought really to fall."
Hamilton supports the idea of a unitary executive as the best means of uniting a nation. The President is accountable to the nation and his selection represents a unity of purpose in decision-making, especially the fair execution of the law and foreign policy. Hamilton promotes the idea that strong nations have strong leaders. To establish a unified nation, the government must create and empower a single executive who works with the council of a Congress, not under the authority of Congress.

2. Term-of-office and constitutional power restrictions, including passage of the **Twenty-Second Amendment**, demonstrates changing presidential roles.

   Commentary: Presidents serve a four-year term by the Constitution. The Twenty-Second Amendment (ratified in 1951) limits presidents to a maximum of two terms.

3. Different perspectives on the presidential role, ranging from a limited to a more expansive interpretation and use of power, continue to be debated in the context of contemporary events.

   Commentary: Political scientists point to several major factors that explain the expansion of presidential (and executive) power. The three examples below may appear on the AP exam.

- **The War Powers Resolution** (1973) allows the President to initiate military activity. Although only Congress is constitutionally empowered to declare war and vote on the military budget, Congress has conceded that presidents should make military commitments of troops or naval vessels. As a reaction to the Vietnam War, Congress passed the War Powers Resolution. It requires presidents to consult with Congress, whenever possible, prior to using military force, and it requires the withdrawal of forces after 60 days unless Congress declares war or grants an extension. Since 1973, presidents have considered the law an unconstitutional infringement on their powers.

- **Executive Agreements:** Presidents negotiate executive agreements with the heads of foreign governments; unlike treaties, executive agreements do not require Senate ratification by two-thirds vote. The table below records the growing use of the agreements.

President	Executive Agreements	Treaties
Richard Nixon (1969–1974)	1,116	180
Gerald Ford (1974–1977)	677	99
Jimmy Carter (1977–1981)	1,169	148
Ronald Reagan (1981–1989)	2,840	125
George H.W. Bush (1989–1993)	1,350	67
Bill Clinton (1933–2001)	2,058	209
George W. Bush (2001–2009)	1,876	131
Barack Obama (2009–2012)	791	21

Source: "The Politics of the Presidency" by Joseph A. Pika.

- **The Expansion of the Bureaucracy**: Some argue that the power of the Presidency has increased, but it is the power of the Executive Branch that has increased. The Founders wrote the Constitution assuming that the President would have the power to fire any federal employee. But since the rise of the Civil Service in the late 19th century, and the unionization of the Federal government starting in the early 1960s, the President has become more of a figure head with the federal bureaucracy being in charge of itself. The regulations created and imposed by these agencies without the consent of the Congress contribute to the growing power of the executive branch. The graph below illustrates the expansion of the bureaucracy.

D. Explain how communication technology has changed the president's relationship with the national constituency and the other branches.

1. The communication impact of the presidency can be demonstrated through such factors as:
   - **Social media**, like twitter and podcasts provide the President direct access to citizens with a rapid response to political issues.

   - **The State of the Union Address** is an annual speech delivered by the president in late January or early February in fulfillment of the constitutional obligation of reporting to Congress the state of the union.

- **Bully Pulpit** - First used by Teddy Roosevelt; the president uses the power of his office to communicate at will to a national audience (through television, radio, and internet streaming) in order to directly persuading the public to support his policies or oppose ideas introduced from political opponents.

Enduring Understanding CONSTITUTIONALISM-5: The design of the judicial branch protects the Supreme Court's independence as a branch of government, and the emergence and use of judicial review remains a powerful judicial practice.

A. Explain the principle of judicial review and how it checks the power of other institutions and state governments.
   1. The foundation for powers of the judicial branch and how its independence checks the power of other institutions and state governments are set forth in:

   - **Article III of the Constitution:** The text of the Constitution does not contain a specific reference to the power of judicial review. However, the power to declare laws unconstitutional is an implied power, derived from Article III. "The judicial power of the United States, shall be vested in one Supreme Court, and in such inferior courts as the Congress may from time to time ordain and establish. . . . The judicial power shall extend to all cases, in law and equity, arising under this Constitution, the laws of the United States, and treaties made, or which shall be made, under their authority. . . . In all cases affecting ambassadors, other public ministers and consuls, and those in which a state shall be party, the Supreme Court shall have original jurisdiction. In all the other cases before mentioned, the Supreme Court shall have appellate jurisdiction, both as to law and fact, with such exceptions, and under such regulations as the Congress shall make."

   - **Federalist No. 78:** Alexander Hamilton proposes that the judiciary has the power to declare legislative acts contrary to the Constitution void. Hamilton purposely ignored the idea that judicial review extends to executive actions.

   - *Marbury v. Madison* (1803): See briefing below.

Main Ideas of Federalist 78 and Critical Passages
• **The judicial branch should have the unique power to interpret of law and declare acts of Congress unconstitutional (judicial review).** "It is far more rational to suppose that the courts were designed to be an intermediate body between the people and the legislature in order, among other things, to keep the latter within the limits assigned to their authority. The interpretation of the laws is the proper and peculiar province of the courts. A constitution is in fact, and must be regarded by the judges as, a fundamental law. It therefore belongs to them to ascertain its meaning as well as the meaning of any particular act proceeding from the legislative body. If there should happen to be an irreconcilable variance between the two, that which has the superior obligation and validity ought, of course; to be preferred; or, in other words, the Constitution ought to be preferred to the statute, the intention of the people to the intention of their agents."
• **The judicial branch must be an independent branch of government. Their independence guarantees independence from the legislature and popular demands.** "If, then, the courts of justice are to be considered as the bulwarks of a limited Constitution against legislative encroachments, this consideration will afford a strong argument for the permanent tenure of judicial offices, since nothing will contribute so much as this to that independent spirit in the judges which must be essential to the faithful performance of so arduous a duty. This independence of the judges is equally requisite to guard the Constitution and the rights of individuals from the effects of those ill humors which the arts of designing men, or the influence of particular conjunctures, sometimes disseminate among the people themselves, and which, though they speedily give place to better information, and more deliberate reflection, have a tendency, in the meantime, to occasion dangerous innovations in the government, and serious oppressions of the minor party in the community.
• **Judges should hold their offices for life as long as they exhibit good behavior.** "That inflexible and uniform adherence to the rights of the Constitution, and of individuals, which we perceive to be indispensable in the courts of justice, can certainly not be expected from judges who hold their offices by a temporary commission. Periodical appointments, however regulated, would in some way or other, be fatal to their necessary independence. If the power of making them was committed either to the executive or legislature there would be danger of an improper complaisance to the branch which possessed it; if to both, there would be an unwillingness to hazard the displeasure of either; if to the people, or to persons chosen by them for the special purpose, there would be too great a disposition to consult popularity to justify a reliance that nothing would be consulted but the Constitution and the laws."
In *Federalist 78*, Alexander Hamilton argues that the independence of the federal courts is essential to an enduring constitution. He proposed that the courts should overturn acts of Congress when they conflict with the Constitution and that justices should be protected against the politics of faction through life terms under good behavior.

Marbury v. Madison (1803)

Constitutional Issue: Judicial Review, Article III, Section 2

Question: Does the Supreme Court have the authority to nullify an act of Congress?

Background

Thomas Jefferson defeated John Adams in the 1800 presidential election. Before Jefferson took office on March 4, 1801, Adams and Congress passed the Judiciary Act 1801, which created new courts, added judges, and gave the president more control over appointment of judges. The Act was an attempt by Adams to frustrate his successor, as he used the act to appoint 16 new circuit judges. The appointees were approved by the Senate, but they were not valid until their commissions were delivered by the Secretary of State John Marshall. William Marbury had been appointed Justice of the Peace in the District of Columbia, but his commission was not delivered. Marbury and three other appointees petitioned the Supreme Court to require the new Secretary of State, James Madison, to deliver the documents.

Holding and Reasoning

Established the principle of judicial review empowering the Supreme Court to nullify an act of the legislative or executive branch that violates the Constitution.

In Marbury v. Madison (1803) the Supreme Court announced for the first time the principle that a court may declare an act of Congress void if it is inconsistent with the Constitution. In writing the decision, John Marshall argued that acts of Congress in conflict with the Constitution are not law and therefore are non-binding to the courts, and that the judiciary's first responsibility is always to uphold the Constitution. If two laws conflict, the court decides which law applies in any given case. Therefore, Marbury never received his job. Though Marbury was entitled to it, the Court was unable to grant it because Section 13 of the Judiciary Act of 1789 conflicted with Article III Section 2 of the U.S. Constitution ("judicial power shall extend to all cases, in law and equity, arising under this Constitution, the laws of the United States").

B. Explain how the exercise of judicial review in conjunction with life tenure can lead to debate about the legitimacy of the Supreme Court's power.

   1. Precedents and *stare decisis* play an important role in judicial decision making.

- **Stare decisis:** The first decision the Supreme Court must make is which cases to decide. The Supreme Court controls its own agenda and while approximately 8,000 cases are submitted each year to the court, only one percent are accepted for review. In a typical year, the Court issues fewer than 100 opinions. The vast majority of cases are settled on the principle of ***stare decisis*** (Latin meaning: let the decision stand). For 99% of submitted cases, the Supreme Court decides that an earlier decision should hold.

- Lower courts are expected to follow the **precedents** of higher courts in their decision making.

   2. Ideological changes in the composition of the Supreme Court due to presidential appointments have led the Court's establishing new or rejecting existing precedents.

   3. Controversial or unpopular Supreme Court decisions can lead to challenges of the Court's legitimacy and power which Congress and the president can address only through future appointments, legislation changing the court's jurisdiction, or refusing to implement decisions.

   4. Political discussion about the Supreme Court's power is illustrated by the ongoing debate over judicial activism versus judicial restraint.

- **Judicial restraint** refers to the belief that judges should limit the exercise of their power. Judges should hesitate to strike down laws unless they are obviously unconstitutional. Judges who practice restraint leave policy decision to the legislatures. Decisions such as those on gay marriage, abortion, and school prayer go beyond their role.

- **Judicial activists** emphasize that the courts may correct social needs especially for the politically and economically disadvantaged. Judges who practice activism generally allow their personal views about public policy to guide their decisions.

C. Explain how other branches in the government can limit the Supreme Court's power.

   1. Restrictions on the Supreme Court occur when:

- Congress begins the process of amending the Constitution to overcome a Supreme Court decision
- Congress can alter the appellate jurisdiction (area of authority) of the Court.

- Congress can clarify an existing law by passing new legislation that effectively overturns the court.
- The President appoints new justices and the Congress confirms them
- The President and states evade or ignore enforcement of Supreme Court decisions

Enduring Understanding COMPETITING POLICY-MAKING INTERESTS-2: The federal bureaucracy is a powerful institution implementing federal policies with sometimes questionable accountability.

A. Explain how the bureaucracy carries out the responsibilities of the federal government.
  1. Tasks performed by departments, agencies, commissions include:
     - **Writing and enforcing regulations**: most agencies responsible for regulation of business develop a set of rules or guidelines and enforce them through its own administration or through the courts.
     - **Issuing fines** on groups and individuals who violate regulations.
     - **Testifying** before a Congressional standing committee responsible for "marking-up" a bill and passing the annual budget for the agency.
     - **Iron triangles:** When bureaucratic agencies, interest groups, and Congressional committees depend on one another and are in close, frequent contact, they form a tight relationship that creates policy protecting their self-interests.

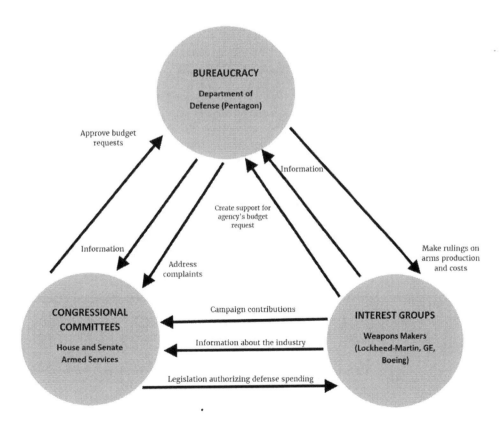

2. Political patronage, civil service, and merit system reforms all impact the effectiveness of the bureaucracy by promoting professionalism, specialization, and neutrality.
   - **Political patronage** refers to granting favors and contracts or making appointments to office in return for political support.
   - **Civil service:** The Pendleton Civil Service Act of 1883 created a system of hiring and promotion based on merit rather than patronage. The purpose of the act was to create a nonpartisan government service.
   - **The merit principle** is the idea that hiring should be based on entrance exams and promotion ratings to produce administration by people with talent and skill.

B. Explain how the federal bureaucracy uses delegated discretionary authority for rule making and implementation.
   1. Discretionary and rule-making authority to implement policy are given to bureaucratic departments, agencies, and commissions, such as:
      - **Department of Homeland Security**: created in 2002 to coordinate national efforts against terrorism
      - **Department of Transportation**: responsible for the national highways and for railroad and airline safety. It also manages Amtrak, the national railroad system, and the Coast Guard.
      - **Department of Veterans Affairs**: helps veterans and their dependents and beneficiaries. Best known for its healthcare system, provides social support services, administers pensions, and promotes the hiring of veterans.
      - **Environmental Protection Agency (EPA)**: An administrative agency created by Congress in 1970 to implement and enforce federal environmental protection laws.
      - **Federal Elections Commission (FEC)**: created by Congress in 1974 to enforce the federal campaign finance law. The FEC has jurisdiction over the financing of campaigns for the U.S. House, the U.S. Senate, the Presidency and the Vice Presidency.
      - **Securities and Exchange Commission (SEC)**: ensures that investors are provided adequate information before buying securities (stocks and bonds) for public investment.

C. Explain how Congress uses its oversight power in its relationship with the executive branch.
   1. Oversight and methods used by Congress to ensure that legislation is implemented as intended are represented by:
      - **Committee hearings** by Congress is one of the checks on the executive branch. Oversight is handled primarily through hearings. Members of committees monitor how a bill is implemented. Experts and witnesses can be subpoenaed to testify before Congress.

- **Power of the purse** refers to the ability of Congress to control an agency's budget. It is the most effective weapon for influencing bureaucratic behavior.

2. As a means to curtail the use of presidential power, congressional oversight serves as a check of executive authorization and appropriation.

D. Explain how the president ensures that executive branch agencies and departments carry out their responsibilities in concert with the goals of the administration.

1. Presidential ideology, authority, and influence affect how executive branch agencies carry out the goals of the administration.

2. Compliance monitoring can pose a challenge to policy implementation.
   Commentary: Some presidential methods of exercising control over bureaucracies include:
   - Appointing the right people to head the agency. Presidents can fire any of bureaucratic executive he appoints.
   - Issuing executive orders.
   - Tinkering with an agency's budget.
   - Reorganizing an agency.

E. Explain the extent to which governmental branches can hold the bureaucracy accountable given the competing interests of Congress, the president, and the federal courts.

1. Formal and informal powers of Congress, the president, and the courts over the bureaucracy are used to maintain its accountability.

Practice Multiple Choice

by Editorial Cartoonist, Kirk Walters; reprinted with permission of The Blade(Toledo, Oh), copyright 2009.

1. Which of the following best describes the message in the political cartoon?
   A. The federal government must implement checks and balances to preserve democracy.
   B. Placing limits on civil liberties is healty for a democratic society
   C. Threats to national security issues are leading to more severe restrictions on civil liberties.
   D. In the United States, no man is above the law.

2. Which of the following constitutional issues is most relevant to the topic of the cartoon?
   A. Freedom of speech
   B. Equal protection rights
   C. The right to privacy
   D. The right to bear arms

Answers: C, B

UNLOCKING AP® U.S. GOVERNMENT

Practice Free Response Question: Type 1 – Concept Application

Experts say the United States is in the throes of an opioid epidemic, as more than two million Americans have become dependent on or abused prescription pain pills and street drugs. Opioids are drugs formulated to replicate the pain reducing properties of opium. They include both legal painkillers like morphine, oxycodone, or hydrocodone prescribed by doctors for acute or chronic pain, as well as illegal drugs like heroin or illicitly made fentanyl. The word "opioid" is derived from the word "opium." During 2016, there were more than 63,600 overdose deaths in the United States, including 42,249 that involved an opioid (66.4%). That's an average of 115 opioid overdose deaths each day.

Cnn.com, June 16, 2018

After reading the scenario, respond to A, B, and C below.

A. Describe a power Congress could use to address the facts in the scenario.

B. In the context of the scenario, explain how the use of congressional power describes in Part A can be affected by its interaction with the bureaucracy.

C. In the context of the scenario, explain how the interaction between Congress and the bureaucracy can be affected by interest groups.

Advance permission required before reproducing

73

Exemplary Answer

A. *To respond to the opioid epidemic, Congress could bring national attention to the crisis by holding hearings, by passing legislation that addressed limits to distribution or penalties for trafficking. Congress could find rehabilitation efforts and education campaigns.*

B. *If Congress passed legislation to regulate opioid distribution, the Drug Enforcement Agency would create specific policies and request monies from Congress to enforce the new act.*

C. *Lobbyists for the pharmaceutical industry would seek to influence both Congress and the bureaucracy so that the legislation and enforcement would not negatively affect sales. They may partner in education and rehabilitation efforts in order to avoid negative publicity.*

Practice Free Response Question: Type 2 -- Quantitative Analysis

Mandatory and Discretionary Spending, 2017

Program	Spending (in billions)	% of mandatory spending
Social Security, Unemployment, and Labor	$1,360	48
Medicare and Health	$1,120	39
Food and Agriculture	$126	4
Veterans' Benefits	$104	4
Transportation	$84	3
Housing and Community	$22	1
Education	$12	<1
Energy and Environment	$10	<1
Military	$10	<1
International Affairs	$4	<1
Science	$1	<1
TOTAL	$2800	

Program	Spending (in billions)	% of discretionary spending
Military	$622.6	54
Veterans' Benefits	$75.4	7
Education	$72.8	6
Government	$69	6
Housing and Community	$68.5	6
Medicare and Health	$58.6	5
International Affairs	$41.4	4
Energy and Environment	$41.3	4
Social Security, Unemployment, and Labor	$31.7	3
Science	$30.7	3
Transportation	$24.7	2

Source: Office of Management and Budget, 2017

Use the data tables to answer the questions.

A. Identify the program that receives the greatest annual expenditure.

B. Describe a similarity or difference in ONE program that appears in both data tables and draw a conclusion about that similarity or difference.

C. Explain how the data as shown in the tables above contribute to the principle of deficit spending.

Exemplary Answer

A. *In the 2017 budget, Social Security, Unemployment, and Labor programs received the largest expenditures by the federal government.*

B. *Military spending represents over half the discretionary budget and a small percentage of the mandatory budget. Military spending would include salaries of the armed forces, purchase of equipment and weapons, and the cost of bases around the world. When the costs of mandatory programs like Medicare continue to rise as the population of elderly grows, policymakers will be pressured to reduce military spending.*

C. *Total government spending on mandatory and discretionary exceeds government revenue each year. This requires the federal government to borrow money to continue its spending levels. The borrowing produces deficit spending. The increasing costs of mandatory programs will continue to put pressure on policymakers to continue deficit spending.*

Practice Free Response Question: Type 2 – Quantitative Analysis

Diplomatic Agreements by Presidential Administration

President	Executive Agreements	Treaties
Richard Nixon (1969-1974)	1,116	180
Gerald Ford (1974-1977)	677	99
Jimmy Carter (1977-1981)	1,169	148
Ronald Reagan (1981-1989)	2,840	125
George H.W. Bush (1989-1993)	1,350	67
Bill Clinton (1933-2001)	2,058	209
George W. Bush (2001-2009)	1,876	131
Barack Obama (2009-2012)	791	21

Source: "The Politics of the Presidency" by Joseph A. Pika.

Use the data table to answer the questions.

A. Identify the administration that conducted the most diplomatic agreements.

B. Describe the pattern between the number of executive agreements and treaties negotiated since 1969 and draw a conclusion about that pattern.

C. Explain how the diplomatic agreements as shown in the table demonstrate executive power.

Exemplary Answer

A. *The Ronald Reagan administration conducted the most diplomatic agreements between 1981 and 1989 – almost 3,000.*

B. *All presidents since 1969 have negotiated significantly more executive agreements than treaties. This data is best explained by the president's power of executive agreements. As chief diplomat, the president can enter into agreements with leaders of other nations (such as trade deals) by an executive agreement. Approval only requires a majority of Congress. Treaties, however, require a two-thirds vote of the Senate. To achieve that level of support is difficult. Therefore, the majority of deals are considered executive agreements.*

C. *The diplomatic agreements recorded in the table demonstrate the President's power as chief diplomat. Only the president has the authority to negotiate legally binding deals with other nations. Many of the conversations are secret – from the public and Congress – until a final deal it reached. These agreements have significant impact on the nation's alliances and trade.*

Practice Free Response Question: Type 3 – Supreme Court Comparison

Directions: Respond to each part of the question below and separate your answers using the A, B, and C indicators. This FRQ is worth four points based on the breakdown below. You have 20-minutes to complete your answer.

- Part A: identify the similarity between the court cases
- Part B: describe factual information about *Shaw v. Reno* (1993)
- Part B: then explain how that information is relevant to *Abbott v. Perez* (2018)
- Part C: describe an interaction between *Abbott v. Perez* (2018) and the states.

Organizations representing African-Americans and Latinos in Texas filed a series of lawsuits in 2011 alleging Texas' congressional and state house plans violated the U.S. Constitution and the Voting Rights Act of 1965. Between 2000 and 2010, Latinos and African-Americans accounted for nearly 90 percent of Texas' population growth, which resulted in the state received four additional congressional seats and required significant changes to both the state house and congressional maps. The citizens (Perez) argued that the state redrew its congressional districts to intentionally dilute Latino and African-American voting strength. Perez argued that Texas should be required to redraw the maps.

In the ensuing case, *Abbott v. Perez* (2018), the court decided 5-4 that there was not enough evidence to say that the Texas legislature intentionally discriminated when they adopted new maps in 2013. The majority opinion concluded that "when the congressional and state legislative districts are reviewed under the proper legal standards, all but one of them, we conclude, are lawful." The justices said that Texas House District 90, which weaves around the north, west, and eastern areas of Fort Worth, is an "impermissible racial gerrymander" because the Texas legislature changed it to manipulate the percent of the district made up of Hispanic and African-American voters.

A. Identify the constitutional clause that is common to both *Abbott v. Perez* (2018) and *Shaw v. Reno* (1993).
B. Based on the constitutional clause identified in part A, explain why the facts of *Shaw v. Reno* (1993) led to a similar holding as *Abbott v. Perez* (2018).
C. Describe an action that states could take to address the court's holding in *Abbott v. Perez* (2018).

Exemplary Answer

A. *The constitutional clause in common to both* Abbott v. Perez *and* Shaw v. Reno *is the equal protection clause of the 14ᵗʰ Amendment which prevents racial discrimination.*

B. *In* Shaw v. Reno, *the Supreme Court held that drawing the lines of congressional districts could not be based primarily on race. Intentionally drawing lines that favor or exclude minorities does not honor citizens' rights to equal protection. Districts must also be compact and not in strange geographic shapes that are not logical. In* Abbott v. Perez, *the court found that as a rule, the new Texas districts were not racially gerrymandered, except for one. And the court ordered the state to correct that district because it was also not compact.*

C. *One way that states could ensure their legislative districts are unconstitutional is to use the decisions of federal courts as guidelines and to collaborate with former judges to make sure their decisions meet the scrutiny of equal protection.*

Practice Free Response Question: Type 3 – Supreme Court Comparison

Directions: Respond to each part of the question below and separate your answers using the A, B, and C indicators. This FRQ is worth four points based on the breakdown below. You have 20-minutes to complete your answer.

- Part A: identify the similarity between the court cases
- Part B: describe factual information about *Baker v. Carr* (1961)
- Part B: then explain how that information is relevant to *Reynolds v. Sims* (1964)
- Part C: describe an interaction between *Reynolds v. Sims* (1964) and Congress.

Alabama Senate and House seats had not been reapportioned among the counties since 1903. Each county had one or more senators and one or more representatives, regardless of population. According to the 1960 Census, the largest Senate district had about 41 times the population of the smallest Senate district, and the largest House district had about 16 times the population of the smallest House district. Alabama justified the districting by arguing that each county should be guaranteed at least one representative.

In the ensuing case, *Reynolds v. Sims* (1964), the Supreme Court held that "the seats in both houses of a bicameral state legislature must be apportioned on a population basis." One Justice declared, "Legislators represent people, not trees or acres.... [M]athematical nicety is not a constitutional requisite" when drawing legislative plans. All that is necessary is that the maps achieve "substantial equality of population among the various districts." Redrawing legislative districts at least every 10 years to reflect population shifts is not constitutionally required, but to redraw them less often "would assuredly be constitutionally suspect."

A. Identify the constitutional clause that is common to both *Reynolds v. Sims* (1964) and *Baker v. Carr* (1961)

B. Based on the constitutional clause identified in part A, explain why the facts of *Baker v. Carr* (1961) led to a similar holding as *Reynolds v. Sims* (1964).

C. Describe a way that Congress is affected by the court's holding in *Reynolds v. Sims* (1964).

Exemplary Answer

A. *The constitutional clause in common to both* Reynolds v. Sims *and* Baker v. Carr *is the equal protection clause of the 14th Amendment which guarantees equality in voting.*

B. *In* Baker v. Carr, *the Supreme Court held that federal courts have the power to hear cases involving reapportionment. Legislative districts must be proportional in terms of population, so that elections represent "one person, one vote." In* Reynolds v. Sims, *the court held that legislative districts must be proportional in terms of population and that states should redraw districts every ten years to account for population changes.*

C. *One way that Congress is affected by the* Sims *decision is that members are increasingly representing more urban constituents than rural and campaigns must appeal to more diverse populations. The census determines how many representatives are awarded to states every ten years, and members of the House must appeal to more than their home constituents because their voter base will change as the national population continues to expand.*

Practice Free Response Question: Type 3 –Supreme Court Comparison

Directions: Respond to each part of the question below and separate your answers using the A, B, and C indicators. This FRQ is worth four points based on the breakdown below. You have 20-minutes to complete your answer.
- Part A: identify the similarity between the court cases
- Part B: describe factual information about *Marbury v. Madison* (1803)
- Part B: then explain how that information is relevant to *U.S. v. Nixon* (1974)
- Part C: describe an interaction between *U.S. v. Nixon* (1974) and the presidency.

During the investigation of President Nixon known as the "Watergate Scandal," seven of the President's closest aides were indicted for participating in a criminal cover-up. The prosecutor sought audio tapes of conversations recorded by Nixon in the Oval Office. The special prosecutor in charge of the case wanted to hear these tapes, but President Nixon did not want to give them up. Nixon claimed that he was immune from the handing them over, claiming "executive privilege," which is the right to withhold information from other government branches to preserve confidential communications within the executive branch or to secure the national interest. His attorneys argued that the courts could not hear the case because it was a dispute within the executive branch over which the courts had no jurisdiction.

In the ensuing case, *U.S. v. Nixon* (1974), the court concluded, 8-0, presidents do enjoy a constitutionally protected executive privilege, but that the privilege was not absolute. The Court decided that in this case, the President's interest in keeping his communications secret was outweighed by the interests of the judiciary in providing a fair trial with full factual disclosure. To support this ruling, the justices cited a prior court decision which declared "it is emphatically the province and duty of the judicial department to say what the law is."

A. Identify the constitutional issue that is common to both *U.S. v. Nixon* (1974) and *Marbury v. Madison* (1803).

B. Based on the constitutional issue identified in part A, explain why the facts of *Marbury v. Madison* (1803) led to a similar holding as *U.S. v. Nixon* (1974).

C. Describe an executive privilege the President could take that would not be subject to the holding in *U.S. v. Nixon* (1974).

Exemplary Answer

A. *The constitutional issue in common to both the* **Nixon** *and* Marbury *cases is judicial review which allows the court to review actions of the executive branch.*

B. *In* Marbury, *the Supreme Court held for the first time that a federal court can declare an act of the President unconstitutional, which means the President's actions are not to be followed. In* **Nixon**, *the court held that the President's actions could not interfere with a fair trial and that information cannot be withheld in a criminal matter. Nixon's power to withhold information was void.*

C. *One action of the President that is not subject to the Nixon holding is any action that secures the national interest. For example, the President may hold secret negotiations with foreign leaders that cannot be revealed to the public. He may also create military plans with his Joint Chiefs of Staff that cannot be made public, even by the Supreme Court, because that information would jeopardize the security of the American people. These examples are part of executive privilege.*

FRQ 4: Argumentative Essay

Develop an argument that explains if the Constitution effectively created three co-equal branches of government.

In your essay, you must:
- Present a defensible thesis that responds to the prompt and establishes a line of reasoning.

- Support your thesis with at least TWO pieces of accurate and relevant information:
  - At least ONE piece of evidence must be from one of the following foundational documents:
    - U.S. Constitution
    - Federalist No. 70
    - Federalist No. 78
  - Use a second piece of evidence from another foundational document from the list or from your study of the policy making process

- Use reasoning to explain why your evidence supports your thesis

- Respond to an opposing or alternative perspective using refutation, concession, or rebuttal

Annotated Answer

The Founders envisioned a national government limited by expressed powers and checks and balances. They created three branches to prevent authoritarian control. While the Constitution has created and maintained a representative democracy, it created a system where the Executive Branch would become significantly more powerful than the other branches, especially in foreign policy but also domestic policy-making. **[Thesis]**

In Federalist 70, Hamilton supports the idea of a strong unitary executive as the best means of uniting a nation, while the Congress remained numerous and separated into two houses. To Hamilton, the President is accountable to the nation not the other branches and his selection represents a unity of purpose in decision. As Commander-in-Chief, the president determines the deployment of one million troops and their length of stay. As Chief Diplomat, he alone is responsible for negotiating treaties and if his decisions cannot be supported by a two-thirds vote, he can use executive agreements that only require a majority. American participation in NAFTA and the WTO are examples of the dominant power of the president to shape foreign affairs. **[Relevant evidence 1; supports thesis]** *Hamilton believed that a strong nation must have strong leaders. A unified nation must empower a single executive that worked with a Congress but not under their authority.* **[Reasoning]**

Executive agreements also shape the national economy. But nothing compares to presidential influence more than his central power – to execute the laws of the nation. The President's control of a bureaucracy of almost 4 million employees decides the fate of every American (the IRS), every business (Federal Trade Commission) and the criminal justice system (Department of Justice). Presidents can make enforcement a priority or ignore it. His appointment of 3,000 senior heads of executive agencies allows him to guide the enforcement process. **[Relevant evidence 2]** *A nation of laws is only effective when those laws are consistently enforced.*

Some political scientists argue that Congress is the most powerful branch because it holds the ultimate power of making law. But the legislative process is so intentionally divided and lengthy that strong authority is needed to pass the most significant legislation. The most significant bill considered each year is the annual budget. It is written by the President's Office of Management and Budget and significant changes to it are subject to a presidential veto. Clearly, the President wields greater power. And while others argue that the courts exercise the most power, the President has the authority to reshape the courts with his appointment power. More than 70% of his judicial appointments are approved. **[Alternative Perspective]**

UNIT 3: CIVIL LIBERTIES AND CIVIL RIGHTS

Enduring Understanding LIBERTY AND ORDER-2: Provisions if the U.S. Constitution's Bill of Rights are continually being interpreted to balance the power of government and the civil liberties of individuals.

A. Explain how the U.S. Constitution protects individual liberties and rights.

　1. The **U.S. Constitution** includes a **Bill of Rights** specifically designed to protect individual liberties and rights.

Amendment	Civil Liberties	Connection to SCOTUS case
First	Speech, press, assembly, petition, religious expression, protection against state establishment of religion	Engel v. Vitale (establishment clause) Wisconsin v Yoder (free exercise) Tinker v Des Moines (symbolic speech) NY Times v. U.S. (free press) Schenck v U.S. (free speech)
Second	Bear arms	McDonald v. Chicago (gun ownership)
Third	No quartering of soldiers in citizen homes	
Fourth	No unreasonable searches or seizures; exclusionary rule	
Fifth	Self-incrimination, double-jeopardy, grand jury indictment; just compensation for eminent domain	
Sixth	Right to counsel, public trial, confront witnesses, impartial and speedy trial	Gideon v. Wainwright (right to counsel)
Seventh	Civil jury trial	
Eighth	No cruel and unusual punishment; no excessive fines or bail	
Ninth	Additional rights are retained by the people (Privacy; confidentiality; own property, etc.)	Roe v. Wade (privacy)
Tenth	Reserved powers of the states and people	

2. Civil liberties are constitutionally established guarantees and freedoms that protect citizens, opinion, and property against arbitrary government interference.

3. The application of the **Bill of Rights** is continuously interpreted by the courts.

B. Describe the rights protected in the Bill of Rights.
   1. The **Bill of Rights** consists of the first ten amendments to the **Constitution**, which enumerates the liberties and rights of individuals.

C. Explain the extent to which the Supreme Court's interpretation of the First and Second Amendments reflects a commitment to individual liberty.
   1. The interpretation and application of the **First Amendment's** establishment and free exercise clauses reflect an ongoing debate over balancing majoritarian religious practice and free exercise, as represented by cases such as:
      - *Engel v Vitale* (1962), which declared school sponsoring of religious activities violates the establishment clause.
      - *Wisconsin v Yoder* (1972), which held that compelling Amish students to attend school past the eighth grade violates the free exercise clause.

   2. The Supreme Court has held that symbolic speech is protected by the First Amendment, demonstrated by *Tinker v Des Moines Independent Community School District* (1969), in which the court ruled that public school students could wear black armbands in school to protest the Vietnam War.

   3. Efforts to balance social order and individual freedom are reflected in interpretations of the First Amendment that limit speech, including:
      - Time, place, and manner regulations
      - Defamatory, offensive, and obscene statements and gestures
      - That which creates a "clear and present danger" based on the ruling in *Schenck v United States* (1919)

   4. In *New York Times Co. v. United States* (1971), the Supreme Court bolstered the freedom of press, establishing a "heavy presumption against prior restraint" even in cases involving national security.

Engel v. Vitale (1962)

Constitutional Issue: Establishment Clause, First Amendment

Question: Can state legislation can require principals, teachers and students to begin the day with prayers that are sponsored and written by the state.

Background

At the beginning of each school day, students in New York state would recite the Pledge of Allegiance and a Prayer. It read: "Almighty God, we acknowledge our dependence upon thee, and beg they blessings upon us, our teacher, and our country." The nondenominational prayer was written by the New York Board of Regents. Steven Engel, representing the parents of 10 students who objected to the recitation of prayer, argued that it violated of the establishment clause of the 1st amendment which was applied to the states through the Fourteenth Amendment. William Vitale, president of the school board argued that the prayer was voluntary and therefore not in violation of the First Amendment.

Holding and Reasoning

School sponsorship of religious activities violates the establishment clause.

The Supreme Court held in a 6-1 ruling (two justices did not participate) that prayers written by the state contradicted the Establishment Clause and therefore violated the U.S. Constitution. The court held that the prayer breached the constitutional wall of separation between church and state.

The majority opinion stated "in this country, it is no part of the business of government to compose official prayers for any group of the American people…. It is a matter of history that this very practice of establishing governmentally composed prayers for religious services was one of the reasons which caused many of our early colonists to leave England and seek religious freedom in America."

Because of the prohibition of the First Amendment against the enactment of any law "respecting an establishment of religion," which is made applicable to the States by the Fourteenth Amendment, state officials may not compose an official state prayer and require that it be recited in the public schools of the State at the beginning of each school day, even if the prayer is denominationally neutral and students may remain silent or be excused from the room while the prayer is being recited.

Wisconsin v Yoder (1972)

Constitutional Issue: Free exercise clause, First Amendment; Due Process clause of the Fourteenth Amendment

Question: Does a state law requiring children to attend school until the age of 16 violate Amish rights under the free exercise of religion clause of the First Amendment?

Background

Wisconsin law required all children to attend public schools until age 16. Jonas Yoder and two other Amish refused to send their children to such schools after the eighth grade, arguing that high school attendance was contrary to their religious beliefs. The evidence showed that the Amish did provide informal vocational education to their children after eighth grade; that Yoder sincerely believed that high school attendance was contrary to the religion; and that they believed the law endangered their own salvation and that of their children. The Amish also believe that high school education takes children away from their community during the formative adolescent period when the children should be acquiring Amish attitudes toward manual work and attaining specific skills needed to perform the adult role of an Amish farmer or housewife. They were prosecuted under the Wisconsin mandatory attendance law.

Holding and Reasoning
Compelling Amish students to attend school past the eighth grade violates the free exercise clause.

In a 6–1 decision, the Supreme Court held that the First Amendment's free exercise of religion clause prevents a state from compelling Amish children to attend school to the age of 16. The majority opinion cited an expert who testified that if the Amish children were required to attend public high schools, the conflict between the worldly values of a secular society and the non-worldly values of a religious society would do them psychological harm. The experts further testified that, torn between state law and demands of their religion, the children might leave their church which could mean the end of the Amish community. In addition, the opinion pointed out that records showed that most Amish children became self-sufficient members of society with excellent records as law-abiding citizens. The Amish, he stated, instilled social and political responsibilities of citizenship in their children, and records disclosed that the Amish had never been known to commit crimes, to receive public assistance, or to be unemployed. The court affirmed, deciding that Wisconsin's compulsory school attendance law unduly burdened the Free Exercise Clause of the First Amendment by forcing Amish parents to send their children to public school after the eighth grade, which violated core Amish religious beliefs requiring them to remain "aloof from the world."

Tinker v. Des Moines Independent Community School District (1969)

Constitutional Issue: First Amendment, freedom of speech (symbolic)

Question: Does a prohibition against the wearing of armbands in public school, as a form of symbolic protest, violate the students' freedom of speech protections guaranteed by the First Amendment?

Background

John and Mary Beth Tinker attended public school in Des Moines, Iowa. In December of 1965 a community group in Des Moines decided to protest American involvement in the Vietnam War by wearing black armbands. The Tinkers agreed to wear their black armbands to school. However, principals in the school district, aware of the students' plans created a rule that any student wearing an armband to school would be suspended unless the student removed the armband. After refusing to take the armbands off, John and Mary Beth Tinker were sent home by the principal. Their suspension lasted until they agreed to come back to school without the armbands. During their suspension the students' parents sued the school for violating their children's right to free speech. Their appeals ultimately were heard by the Supreme Court.

The question of what kind of speech or action is protected under the First Amendment has been considered many times by the Supreme Court. Generally, the Court has held that the First Amendment protects adult symbolic speech that does not harm or threaten to harm. However, at the time of *Tinker*, it was unclear whether students' rights in this area were different. The Court had to consider two questions: were the armbands a form of symbolic speech protected by the First Amendment? And if so, did the school district have the power to restrict that speech in the interest of maintaining order in the school?

Holding and Reasoning

Public school students have the right to wear armbands in school to protest war.

In a 7-2 decision, the Court found that the armbands were "pure speech" and that the school's action was unconstitutional. The Court found that the school had not demonstrated that the armbands caused "a material and substantial interference with schoolwork or discipline." The majority ruled that students retain their constitutional right of freedom of speech while in public school. The Court noted that the school district had not banned all political symbols but had instead "singled out" the armbands for prohibition. In other words, the limiting of speech was not content-neutral – a test the Supreme Court uses when deciding some First Amendment cases.

Schenck v. U.S. (1919)

Constitutional Issue: First Amendment, freedom of speech

Question: Is anti-war speech that obstructs the recruitment of the armed forces during war protected speech under the First Amendment?

Background

The Petitioner, Schenck (Petitioner), distributed mailers that opposed the draft during World War I. The Petitioner sent mailers to all men that were drafted into the war. The flyer consisted of 2 pages that implored the draftees to "Assert Your Rights" and standup against the draft. The Respondent, Charles T. Schenck, general secretary of the U.S. Socialist Party, opposed the implementation of a military draft during World War I. The party printed and distributed some 15,000 leaflets that called for men who were drafted to resist military service. The U.S. government charged Schenck with conspiracy to violate the Espionage Act of 1917 by encouraging insubordination in the military. Congress passed act to make illegal "the interference with the operation or success of the military ... or to promote the success of its enemies...[or] willfully cause or attempt to cause ... refusal of duty in the military or naval forces of the United States." Schenck's counsel argued that the Espionage Act was unconstitutional and that his client was simply exercising his freedom of speech guaranteed by the First Amendment.

Holding and Reasoning
Speech creating a "clear and present danger" is not protected by the First Amendment.

The Supreme Court held in a unanimous ruling (9-0) that the Espionage Act did not violate the First Amendment and was an appropriate exercise of Congress' wartime authority. The decision argued that the courts owe greater deference to the government during wartime, even when constitutional rights were at stake. The First Amendment does not protect speech that creates a clear and present danger to an individual or nation. The justices reasoned that the widespread dissemination of the leaflets was sufficiently likely to disrupt the conscription process. The justices famously compared the leaflets to shouting "Fire!" in a crowded theatre, which is not permitted under the First Amendment. "Words which, ordinarily and in many places, would be within the freedom of speech protected by the First Amendment may become subject to prohibition when of such a nature and used in such circumstances as to create a clear and present danger that they will bring about the substantive evils which Congress has a right to prevent."

New York Times Co v. United States (1971)

Constitutional Issue: First Amendment, freedom of press

Question: Can the U.S. government prevent the New York Times and the Washington Post from printing the Pentagon Papers under the guide of national security? Is "prior restraint" constitutional?

Background

U.S. military analyst Daniel Ellsberg copied more than 7000 pages of documents that revealed the history of the U.S. government's actions in the Vietnam War. These "Pentagon Papers" exposed government knowledge that the war would cost more lives than the public was being told, and that the war was being escalated even as the President had said it was close to ending.

Ellsberg believed that Americans needed to know what was in the reports and decided to break several laws by giving copies to the *New York Times* and the *Washington Post* newspapers. The U.S. government immediately obtained a court order preventing the printing of more documents, arguing that publishing the material threatened national security. This was the first time in American history that the government had successfully ordered a prior restraint – an order that news be censored ahead of publication.

Holding and Reasoning
The First Amendment protects the press against "prior restraint" by government even in cases involving national security.

The Supreme Court held in a 6-3 ruling that the prior restraint was unconstitutional. The Court ruled 6-3 in *New York Times v. United States* that the prior restraint was unconstitutional. The majority opinion argued that "only a free and unrestrained press can effectively expose deception in government...In revealing the workings of government that led to the Vietnam War, the newspapers nobly did that which the Founders hoped and trusted they would do." The court dismissed the claim that publication threated national security. "The word 'security' is a broad, vague generality whose contours should not be invoked to abrogate the fundamental law embodied in the First Amendment." Any prior restraint of information is necessarily a repeal of the constitutionally protected rights of the press. The First Amendment freedom of the press should be afforded the greatest protection. An injunction that seeks to proactively put down speech is impermissible, unless imminent harm can be proven.

5. The Supreme Court's decisions on the **Second Amendment** rest upon its constitutional interpretation of <u>individual</u> liberty.

   Commentary: Some political scientists argue that the Second Amendment protects a collective, rather than an individual, right to "keep and bear arms." As a result, they conclude that the federal government can prohibit the private ownership of firearms and allowing access to weapons only to those who belong to the National Guard — the descendant of early-American militia. But in the 2008 case of *District of Columbia v. Heller*, the Supreme Court ruled that the Second Amendment protects the rights of the individual.

D. Explain how the Supreme Court has attempted to balance claims of individual freedom with laws and enforcement procedures that promote public order and safety.

   1. Court decisions defining cruel and unusual punishment involve interpretation of the Eighth Amendment and its application to state death penalty statutes over time.

      Commentary: The debate over the death penalty as cruel and unusual punishment dates back to the Founding Fathers, and recent court decisions have confirmed the practice as constitutional, but with limitations. The Eighth Amendment states that, "Excessive bail shall not be required, nor excessive fines imposed, nor cruel and unusual punishments inflicted." Since 1890, Justices have ruled that "punishments are cruel when they involve torture or a lingering death; but the punishment of death is not cruel, within the meaning of that word as used in the Constitution." The Congressional Research Service concluded in its analysis of Eighth Amendment cases that, "the proper approach to an interpretation of this provision has been one of the major points of difference among the Justices in the capital punishment cases." In later years, the Court has excluded certain classes of people from capital punishment, including the mentally handicapped and juveniles. It also eliminated rape and felony murder as capital crimes.

   2. The debate about the Second and Fourth Amendments involves concerns about public safety and whether or not the government regulation of firearms or collection of digital metadata promotes or interferes with public safety and individual rights.

Enduring Understanding LIBERTY AND ORDER-3: Protections of the Bill of Rights have been selectively incorporated by way of the Fourteenth Amendment's due process clause to prevent state infringement of basic liberties.

A. Explain the implication of the doctrine of selective incorporation.
1. The doctrine of selective incorporation has imposed on states regulation of civil rights and liberties as represented by:

- *McDonald v. Chicago* (2010), which ruled the **Second Amendment's** right to keep and bear arms for self-defense in one's home is applicable to the states through the **Fourteenth Amendment**.

Commentary: Legal scholars agree that the Bill of Rights was adopted as a check on federal, not state, authority. When the Fourteenth Amendment was ratified in 1868, the Supreme Court began to hold that the Bill of Rights may be incorporated to the states through the Due Process Clause. States cannot enact laws that take away the constitutional rights of American citizens that are enshrined in the Bill of Rights. In 1925, the Supreme Court, for the first time, relied on the Fourteenth Amendment to find that a state government must respect some First Amendment rights (*Gitlow* v. *New York*).

The Supreme Court gradually applied most of the Bill of Rights to the states, particularly during the 1960s and 1970s, developing **the concept of the incorporation doctrine**. At the present time, only the Third and Seventh Amendments and the grand jury requirement of the Fifth Amendment have not been applied specifically to the states.

McDonald v. Chicago (2010)

Constitutional Issue: Second Amendment, right to bear arms

Question: Does the Second Amendment right to bear arms apply to the states through the Due Process Clause of the Fourteenth Amendment?

Background

Otis McDonald, a retired maintenance engineer, wanted to purchase a handgun for personal protection in his home. McDonald had grown frustrated with increasing levels of crime, having been the victim of theft or break-ins on several occasions. Already the legal owner of both rifles and shotguns, Mr. McDonald believed he could better protect himself in close quarters with the aid of a handgun. The city of Chicago passed an ordinance requiring all handguns be registered with the city in order for ownership to be legal. At the same time, the City had refused to issue any new permits for almost thirty years. In effect, the restrictions effectively banned all legal handgun possession and deprived Mr. McDonald of the right to own a handgun legally. McDonald joined together with other plaintiffs to bring a lawsuit, claiming that the near-total ban on handguns deprived them of the right to keep and bear arms under the Second Amendment. McDonald was confident that the courts would rule against the Chicago ban based on the 2008 Supreme Court decision in U.S. v. Heller. In that case, the court overturned a handgun ban in the District of Columbia. Mr. McDonald argued that the Second Amendment should also apply to the states.

Holding and Reasoning

The Second Amendment right to keep and bear arms for self-defense is applicable to the states through the Due Process Clause of the Fourteenth Amendment.

The Supreme Court held in a 5-4 ruling that self-defense is a basic right and was the central component of the Second Amendment. The Court recognized that the Second Amendment right applied to handguns, which were the preferred firearm to keep and use for protection of one's home and family. The majority opinion explained that the Bill of Rights limited the authority of the federal government by protecting certain enumerated rights specifically. However, with the adoption of the Fourteenth Amendment the Court had held that most of the guarantees of the Bill of Rights had been incorporated to the States through the Due Process Clause. While the Court had never previously held the Second Amendment incorporated, they opted to do so here by citing the fundamental nature of self-defense and necessity of the right to bear arms to guarantee self-protection. The Court emphasized that the Second Amendment guarantee of the right to keep and bear arms was an individual liberty and extended those protections by limiting the right of states to prohibit individual firearm ownership.

B. Explain the extent to which states are limited by the due process clause from infringing upon individual rights.

1. The Supreme Court has on occasion ruled in favor of states' power to restrict individual liberty; for example, when speech can be shown to increase the danger to public safety.

2. The Miranda rule involves the interpretation and application of accused persons' due process rights as protected by the Fifth and Sixth Amendments, yet the Supreme Court has sanctioned a public safety exception that allows unwarned interrogation to stand as direct evidence in court.

   Commentary: The Fifth Amendment protects citizens against forced self-incrimination. Suspects cannot be forced to provide evidence that can be used against them. The *Miranda* v. *Arizona* (1966) decision required police to inform suspects of their constitutional rights before questioning. "You have the right to remain silent. Anything you say can and will be used against you in a court of law. You have the right to an attorney. If you cannot afford an attorney, one will be provided for you."

3. Pretrial rights of the accused and prohibition of unreasonable searches and seizures are intended to ensure that citizen liberties are not eclipsed by the need for social order and security, including:
   - The right to legal counsel, a speedy trial, and an impartial jury
   - Protection against warrantless searches of phone data under the **Fourth Amendment.**
   - Limitation placed on bulk collection of telecommunication metadata. In response to 9/11, Congress passed the **Patriot Act (2001)** which increased the government's surveillance powers to look at records of an individual's activity being held by third parties (internet, cell providers) without notice to the owner. In 2015, the National Security Agency (Executive Branch) stopped its bulk collection of telephony metadata once authorized under the USA Patriot Act. Under the **USA Freedom Act of 2015**, Congress allows the storage of data from phone providers but requires a valid search warrant before the records are searched by authorities.

4. The due process clause has been applied to guarantee the right to an attorney and protection from unreasonable searches and seizures, as represented by:
   - *Gideon v Wainwright* (1963), which guaranteed the right to an attorney for the poor.
   - The exclusionary rule, which stipulated that evidence illegally seized by law enforcement officers in violation of the suspect's **Fourth Amendment** right to be free of unreasonable searches and seizures cannot be used against that suspect in criminal prosecution.

Gideon v. Wainwright (1963)

Constitutional Issue: Right to Counsel (6th Amendment) and Due Process (14th Amendment)

Question: Are the states obligated to appoint a lawyer for indigent (poor) defendants?

Background

Clarence Earl Gideon, a man with an eighth-grade education who ran away from home when he was in middle school, was a drifter, spending time in and out of prisons for nonviolent crimes. He was charged with breaking into a bar in Panama City, Florida, with intent to commit a misdemeanor – a felony under Florida law. At trial, Gideon appeared in court without an attorney. He asked the judge to appoint an attorney for him because he could not afford one. The judge denied his request because Florida law only permitted appointment of counsel for poor defendants charged with capital offenses. Gideon represented himself including making an opening statement to the jury, cross-examining the prosecution's witnesses and presented his own witnesses. The jury found Gideon guilty and he was sentenced to five years imprisonment. Gideon filed a petition in the Supreme Court of the United States. The Court agreed to hear the case to resolve the question of whether the right to counsel guaranteed under the Sixth Amendment of the Constitution applies to defendants in state court.

Holding and Reasoning
States must guarantee the indigent the right to an attorney.

The Supreme Court held in a 9-0 ruling that the Sixth Amendment's guarantee of counsel is a fundamental right essential to a fair trial and applies the states through the Due Process Clause of the Fourteenth Amendment. The majority opinion stated: "reason and reflection require us to recognize that in our adversary system of criminal justice, any person hauled into court, who is too poor to hire a lawyer, cannot be assured a fair trial unless counsel is provided for him." He further wrote that the "noble ideal" of "fair trials before impartial tribunals in which ever defendant stands equal before the law . . . cannot be realized if the poor man charged with crime has to face his accusers without a lawyer to assist him."

5. While a right to privacy is not explicitly named in the Constitution, the Supreme Court has interpreted the due process clause to protect the right of privacy from state infringement. The interpretation of the due process clause has been the subject of controversy, such as has resulted from:

- ***Roe v Wade*** (1973), which extended the right of privacy to a woman's decision to have an abortion while recognizing compelling state interests in potential life and maternal health.

Roe v. Wade (1973)

Constitutional Issue: Ninth Amendment, right to privacy; Fourteenth Amendment, due process

Question: Does the Texas anti-abortion law violate a pregnant woman's right to privacy?

Background

Jane Roe was a single pregnant woman representing a class action suit against a Texas abortion law that made procuring an abortion a crime except for the purpose of saving the life of the mother. The purposes for the law were to protect pregnant woman from a hazardous procedure and to protect prenatal life. Roe argued that she was unmarried and pregnant, and that she was unable to receive a legal abortion by a licensed physician because her life was not threatened by the continuation of her pregnancy. She was also unable to afford to travel to another state to obtain a legal abortion. She sued on behalf of herself and all other women similarly situated, claiming that the statutes were unconstitutionally vague and violated her right of personal privacy, protected by the Ninth and Fourteenth Amendments.

Holding and Reasoning
The Ninth Amendment "right to privacy" extends to a woman's decision to have an abortion.

The Supreme Court held in a 7-2 ruling that a woman's choice whether to have an abortion is protected by her right to privacy. The justices asserted that the Fourteenth Amendment, which prohibits states from "depriv[ing] any person of ... liberty ... without due process of law," protected a fundamental right to privacy. The right of a woman to choose to have an abortion fell within this fundamental right to privacy and was protected by the Constitution. In the case of *Griswold* v. *Connecticut* (1965), the Supreme Court said that Connecticut could not stop married couples from getting birth control. The Court said that families have a right to privacy in their decisions about having children and sexual relationships. The Court said that privacy was a basic value that is important for all the rights in the Bill of Rights. This right is fundamental <u>but not absolute</u>. Striking a balance between a woman's right to privacy and a state's interests, the Court set up a framework laying out when states could regulate and even prohibit abortions.

Although the fetus is not a "person" under the 14th amendment, a state has an interest in safeguarding health of the mother and in the protection of "potential life." With respect to the interest in the health of the mother, the state's interest becomes "compelling" at the end of the first trimester because it becomes significantly more unsafe to perform an abortion after the first trimester. With respect to the interest in the potential life, the "compelling" point is at the viability of the fetus; when it becomes capable of meaningful life outside the mother's womb - about 7 months. In deciding for Roe, the Supreme Court invalidated any state laws that prohibited first trimester abortions.

Enduring Understanding CIVIC PARTICIPATION IN A REPRESENTATIVE DEMOCRACY-1: The Fourteenth Amendment's equal protection clause as well as other constitutional provision have often been used to support the advancement of equality.

A. Explain how constitutional provisions have supported and motivated social movements.

1. Civil rights protect individuals from discrimination based on characteristics such as race, national origin, religion, and sex; these rights are guaranteed to all citizens under the due process and equal protection clauses of the **U.S. Constitution**, as well as acts of Congress.

   Commentary: The struggle for equal rights has been the longest conflict in American history. Traditionally disadvantaged groups demand more equality as a **civil right** – policies that extend basic rights to groups historically subject to discrimination. Constitutionally, civil rights involve interpreting law and applying the **equal protection clause** of the 5th Amendment to national issues and the **equal protection clause** of the 14th Amendment to state issues. Today, debates over inequality focus on age, disability, and sexual preference discrimination as well as racial discrimination. The only place in which the idea of equality appears in the Constitution is in the **Fourteenth Amendment,** which prohibits the states from denying "equal protection of the laws" to any person. It was not until the Civil Rights movement, started by the *Brown v. Board* decision, that the Fourteenth Amendment was applied to the states to guarantee rights for disadvantaged groups.

2. The leadership and events associated with civil, women's, and LGBTQ rights are evidence of how the equal protection clause can support and motivate social movements, as represented by:

   - **The National Organization for Women (NOW) and the women's rights movement.** The civil rights movement of the 1950s and 1960s inspired the creation of NOW which advocated for Congress, not the courts, to recognize civil rights for women. The Civil Rights Act of 1964 banned sex discrimination in employment. In 1972, the Equal Employment Opportunity Commission (EEOC) was given the power to sue employers suspected of illegal sex discrimination. Title IX of the Education Act of 1972 forbade sex discrimination in federally funded education programs, including athletics.

   - **The pro-life (anti-abortion) movement** argues that human life begins at conception and a fetus has a legal guarantee to equal protection of life under the law. A human life amendment to the U.S. Constitution and legislation enforcing it can end abortion in this country but is unlikely. In the meantime, the pro-life movement advocates presidential nominations that will overturn *Roe v. Wade.*

- Dr. Martin Luther King's ***"Letter from a Birmingham Jail"*** and the civil rights movement of the 1960s.

Main Ideas of "Letter from a Birmingham Jail" and Critical Passages
• **King argues that laws must be based on a moral sense in order to be just; law and morality cannot be seen as separate pursuits or areas. He frames his argument in terms similar to the principles of the Declaration (natural law) and the "equal protection" clause of the 14th Amendment.** "Injustice anywhere is a threat to justice everywhere…. I have yet to engage in a direct action campaign that was 'well timed' in the view of those who have not suffered unduly from the disease of segregation. For years now I have heard the word "Wait!" It rings in the ear of every Negro with piercing familiarity. This "Wait" has almost always meant "Never." We must come to see, with one of our distinguished jurists, that 'justice too long delayed is justice denied'…. An unjust law is a human law that is not rooted in eternal law and natural law. Any law that uplifts human personality is just. Any law that degrades human personality is unjust. All segregation statutes are unjust because segregation distorts the soul and damages the personality. It gives the segregator a false sense of superiority and the segregated a false sense of inferiority…Thus it is that I can urge men to obey the 1954 decision of the Supreme Court, for it is morally right; and I can urge them to disobey segregation ordinances, for they are morally wrong." • **Individuals must actively seek to create the world they want and fulfill the national destiny of human dignity for all.** "Actually, time itself is neutral; it can be used either destructively or constructively. More and more I feel that the people of ill will have used time much more effectively than have the people of good will. We will have to repent in this generation not merely for the hateful words and actions of the bad people but for the appalling silence of the good people. Human progress never rolls in on wheels of inevitability; it comes through the tireless efforts of men willing to be co workers with God, and without this hard work, time itself becomes an ally of the forces of social stagnation. We must use time creatively, in the knowledge that the time is always ripe to do right. Now is the time to make real the promise of democracy and transform our pending national elegy into a creative psalm of brotherhood. Now is the time to lift our national policy from the quicksand of racial injustice to the solid rock of human dignity.
King does not refer to the Founding documents as the basis for his call to end segregation through individual action. He prefers to use moral righteousness and history to demonstrate why justice must come for African-Americans. Just as the Declaration of Independence inspired a people to establish a sovereign nation based on a respect for life and individual liberties, this letter inspired President John F. Kennedy to begin the legislative process that resulted in the Civil Rights Act of 1964.

Enduring Understanding COMPETITING POLICY-MAKING INTERESTS-3: Public policy promoting civil rights is influenced by citizen-state interactions and constitutional interpretation over time.

A. Explain how the government has responded to social movements.
1. The government can respond to social movements through court rulings and/or policies:
   - **The Civil Rights Act of 1964** made racial discrimination illegal in hotels, restaurants, and other public places of business. The Act also banned job discrimination, and Congress cut off federal aid to segregated schools.
   - **Title IX of the Education Amendments Act of 1972** banned sex discrimination in federally subsidized education programs, including athletics.
   - **The Voting Rights Act of 1965** prohibited any government from using voting procedures that denied a person the vote on the basis of race or color (literacy tests).

Enduring Understanding CONSTITUTIONALISM-6: The Supreme Court's interpretation of the U.S. Constitution is influenced by the composition of the Court and citizen-state interactions. At times, it has restricted minority rights and, at others, protected them.

A. Explain how the Supreme Court has at times allowed the restriction of the civil rights of minority groups and at other times has protected those rights.
1. Decisions demonstrating that minority rights have been restricted at times and protected at other times include:
   - State laws and Supreme Court holdings restricting African American access to the same restaurants, hotels, schools, etc., as the majority white population based on the "separate but equal" doctrine: *Plessy v. Ferguson* case.
   - **_Brown v Board of Education_** (1954), which declared that race-based school segregation violates the **Fourteenth Amendment's** equal protection clause.
   - The Supreme Court upholding the rights of the majority in cases that limit and prohibit majority-minority districting.

2. The debate on affirmative action includes justices who insist that the **Constitution** is colorblind and those who maintain that it forbids only racial classifications designed to harm minorities, not help them.
   Commentary: Women and minorities generally support **affirmative action** policies that require special efforts in employment, promotion, or school admissions. The goal of affirmative action is to move beyond equal opportunity toward equal results. Supporters argue that increasing the number of women and minorities in desirable jobs is an important social goal. Opponents argue that affirmative action is reverse discrimination, where less qualified people are hired or admitted to universities.

Brown v. Board of Education of Topeka, (1954)

Constitutional Issue: Equal Protection clause, Fourteenth Amendment

Question: Does a state law requiring children to attend school until the age of 16 violate Amish rights under the free exercise of religion clause of the First Amendment?

Background

In Topeka, Kansas, Linda Brown had to walk through a dangerous railroad switchyard to get to the bus stop for the ride to their all-black elementary school. There was a school closer to the Brown's house, but it was only for white students. Racial segregation in schools and other public places was common throughout the South and elsewhere and legally permissible because of the Supreme Court's *Plessy* v. *Ferguson* decision in 1896. In that case, the Court said that as long as segregated facilities were equal in quality, segregation did not violate the Constitution. The Brown family believed that the segregated school system did violate the Fourteenth Amendment guarantee that people will be treated equally under the law.

Holding and Reasoning
Race-based school segregation violates the equal protection clause.

In a 9-0 decision, the Supreme Court established the precedent that "separate-but-equal" education was not equal at all. The court's opinion called public education "the very foundation of good citizenship," not only necessary to prepare children for their future professions and to enable them to actively participate in the democratic process, but that it was also "a principal instrument in awakening the child to cultural values" in their communities. The justices found it unlikely that a child would be successful without a good education. Education was "a right which must be made available to all on equal terms."

The justices then assessed the equality of the facilities provided for the education of African American children against those provided for white children. Ruling that they were substantially equal in "tangible factors" (such as "buildings, curricula, and qualifications of teachers), they concluded that the Court must examine the more subtle, intangible effect of segregation. Here, they argued that separating children solely on the basis of race created a feeling of inferiority in the "hearts and minds" of African American children. Segregating children in public education perpetuated the idea that African American children held a lower status in the community than white children, even if their separate educational facilities were substantially equal in "tangible" factors. This feeling of inferiority reduced the desire to learn and had "a tendency to retard their educational and mental development and to deprive them of some of the benefits they would receive in a racially integrated school system."

Practice Multiple Choice

by Editorial Cartoonist, Kirk Walters; reprinted with permission of The Blade(Toledo, Oh), copyright 2014.

1. Which of the following best describes the message in the political cartoon?
   A. The nation's poor require government programs in order to survive a weak economy.
   B. Republicans are reluctant to expand support for social welfare programs.
   C. Congress is willing to spend more money on unemployment benefits when the need arises.
   D. Democrats must join Republicans to end a financial crisis that threatens American workers.

2. Which of the following ideological perspectives is most consistent with the passage?
   A. Liberal
   B. Conservative
   C. Progressive
   D. Socialist

3. How does the cartoon relate to the principle of limited government?
   A. Government should always increase spending on social issues to help American citizens temporarily.
   B. Government should ignore economic concerns because they are not addressed in the Constitution.
   C. Government should increase taxes on the rich in order to increase spending on the poor.
   D. Government should rely on free-market solutions to economic problems instead of expanding government programs to solve them.

Answers: B,B,D

Practice Free Response Question: Type 3 – Supreme Court Comparison

Directions: Respond to each part of the question below and separate your answers using the A, B, and C indicators. This FRQ is worth four points based on the breakdown below. You have 20-minutes to complete your answer.

- Part A: identify the similarity between the court cases
- Part B: provide factual information about *Engel v. Vitale* (1962)
- Part B: explain how that information is relevant to *Wallace v. Jaffree* (1985)
- Part C: describe an interaction between *Wallace v. Jaffree* (1985) and the public.

Between 1978 and 1982, the state of Alabama passed a series of laws that created a minute of silence for meditation or voluntary prayer, with teachers authorized to recite a prayer with willing students. On behalf of his three children, Ishmael Jaffree filed an injunction restraining the school board from allowing these practices and other forms of religious service.

In the ensuing case, *Wallace v. Jaffree* (1985), the Supreme Court held in a 6-3 decision that the Alabama law was unconstitutional. The majority opinion stated the law lacked an obvious secular purpose and was enacted for the sole purpose of endorsing school prayer at the start of every school day.

A. Identify the constitutional clause that is common to both *Wallace v. Jaffree* (1985) and *Engel v. Vitale* (1962).

B. Based on the constitutional clause identified in part A, explain why the facts of *Engel v. Vitale* (1962) led to a similar holding as in *Wallace v. Jaffree* (1985).

C. Describe an action that students and parents who disagree with the holding in *Wallace v. Jaffree* (1985) could take to limit its impact.

Exemplary Answer

A. *The constitutional issue in common to both* Engel v. Vitale *and* Wallace v. Jaffree *cases is the establishment clause of the First Amendment, which prevents a government from endorsing a religious practice.*

B. *In* Engel, *the Supreme Court held that a school sponsored prayer, written by government officials with dedicated time every day for mandatory prayer violated the establishment clause. In* Wallace v. Jaffree, *the court held a dedicated time in school specifically for prayer also violated the establishment clause, even though the prayer was voluntary.*

C. *Students and parents who disagree with the* Wallace v. Jaffree *decision could volunteer to have prayer before school. See You at the Pole is a voluntary prayer rally popular with some communities. Also, students and parents could lobby their legislature to dedicate a moment of silence without specifying prayer as the reason. As long as participation is voluntary, the law would be constitutional.*

Practice Free Response Question: Type 3 – Supreme Court Comparison

Directions: Respond to each part of the question below and separate your answers using the A, B, and C indicators. This FRQ is worth four points based on the breakdown below. You have 20-minutes to complete your answer.

- Part A: identify the similarity between the court cases
- Part B: describe factual information about *Wisconsin v. Yoder* (1972)
- Part B: then explain how that information is relevant to *Burwell v. Hobby Lobby* (2013).
- Part C: describe an interaction between *Burwell v. Hobby Lobby* (2013) and interest groups.

The Green family owns and operates Hobby Lobby Stores, Inc., a national arts and crafts chain with over 500 stores and over 13,000 employees. The Green family has organized the business around the principles of the Christian faith and has operated the company according to Biblical precepts, one of which is the belief that the use of contraception is immoral. Under the Patient Protection and Affordable Care Act (ACA), employment-based group health care plans must provide certain types of preventative care, such as contraceptive methods. While there are exemptions available for religious employers and non-profit religious institutions, there are no exemptions available for for-profit institutions such as Hobby Lobby Stores, Inc.

The Green family challenged the contraception requirement, appealing the case to the Supreme Court. They argued that the requirement to cover contraception violates their personal freedoms. In a 5-4 decision, the Supreme Court held that the Religious Freedom Restoration Act permits for-profit corporations owned by a family to refuse, on religious grounds, to pay for legally mandated contraceptives in their employees' health insurance plans. The court embraced the view that closely held for-profit corporations are legal "persons" under the RFRA and are therefore capable of exercising individual liberties.

A. Identify the constitutional clause that is common to both *Burwell v. Hobby Lobby* (2013) and *Wisconsin v. Yoder* (1972).

B. Based on the constitutional clause identified in part A, explain why the facts of *Wisconsin v. Yoder* (1972) led to a holding different than the holding of *Burwell v. Hobby Lobby* (2013).

C. Describe an action that an interest group could take to address the court's holding in *Burwell v. Hobby Lobby* (2013).

Exemplary Answer

A. *The constitutional issue in common to both the* Yoder *and* Hobby Lobby *cases is the free exercise clause of the First Amendment, which allows individuals the freedom to follow their religious convictions without state interference.*

B. *In* Yoder, *the Supreme Court held that requiring Amish students to attend public school past the eighth grade violated the free exercise clause. The Amish had a long tradition of their religious beliefs respecting the laws of the U.S. and of raising their children as responsible citizens. To force the Amish to violate their child raising practices would be psychologically damaging. In* Hobby Lobby, *the court held requiring a family to make contraceptives available to employees violated their right to free exercise over their religious beliefs and management of a business.*

C. *An interest group like Planned Parenthood and other non-profit organizations could raise awareness for their causes by providing contraceptives to Hobby Lobby employees. The outreach would raise attention in the media and be a win-win for the employees and the interest group.*

Practice Free Response Question: Type 3 –Supreme Court Comparison

Directions: Respond to each part of the question below and separate your answers using the A, B, and C indicators. This FRQ is worth four points based on the breakdown below. You have 20-minutes to complete your answer.

- Part A: identify the similarity between the court cases
- Part B: provide factual information about *Tinker vs Des Moines* (1969)
- Part B: explain how that information is relevant to *Texas v. Johnson* (1989)
- Part C: describe an interaction between *Texas v. Johnson* (1989) and Congress.

During the Republican National Convention in 1984, Gregory Lee Johnson participated in a group political demonstration. The demonstrators were opposed to nuclear weapons. One demonstrator took an American flag from a flagpole and gave it to Johnson who set it on fire. While the flag burned, protesters chanted "America, the red, white, and blue, we spit on you." There were no injuries or threats of injury during the demonstration. Johnson was arrested and charged with violating a Texas state law that banned the desecration of the American flag in a way that would seriously offend one or more persons likely to observe his action.

Johnson argued he was merely exercising personal liberty; the state of Texas argued it had an interest in preserving the flag as a symbol of national unity. In the ensuing case, *Texas v. Johnson* (1989), the Court agreed with Johnson (5-4) and struck down the Texas law. Burning a U.S. flag in protest was expressive conduct protected by the Bill of Rights.

A. Identify the constitutional clause that is common to both *Texas v. Johnson* (1989) and *Tinker vs Des Moines* (1969).

B. Based on the constitutional clause identified in part A, explain why the facts of *Tinker vs Des Moines* (1969) led to a holding similar to *Texas v. Johnson* (1989).

C. Describe an action that the U.S. Congress could take to overturn the court's holding in *Texas v. Johnson* (1989).

Exemplary Answer

A. *The constitutional issue in common to both the* Johnson *and* Tinker *cases is the freedom of speech protection in the First Amendment.*

B. *In* Tinker, *the Supreme Court held that student armbands in protest of the Vietnam War was symbolic speech and the school had not demonstrated that they had disrupted education activities. In* Johnson, *the court also held that the flag burning was symbolic speech and did not damage property or harm anyone.*

C. *Congress could overturn the decision by sponsoring a constitutional amendment. If two-thirds of the U.S. Congress decided to make flag burning a crime, the proposal would be sent to the states for ratification. If three-fourths of the states approved, the proposal would become the 28th amendment to the Constitution.*

Practice Free Response Question: Type 3 – Supreme Court Comparison

Directions: Respond to each part of the question below and separate your answers using the A, B, and C indicators. This FRQ is worth four points based on the breakdown below. You have 20-minutes to complete your answer.

- Part A: identify the similarity between the court cases
- Part B: provide factual information about *Tinker vs Des Moines* (1969)
- Part B: explain how that information is relevant to *Bethel School District v. Fraser* (1986)
- Part C: describe an interaction between *Bethel School District v. Fraser* (1986) and the public.

Mathew Fraser, a senior at Bethel High School in Washington state, spoke to a school assembly to nominate a classmate for an office in student government. His speech was filled with sexual references and a graphic sexual metaphor, but it contained no obscenities. As part of its disciplinary code, Bethel High School enforced a rule prohibiting conduct which "substantially interferes with the educational process . . . including the use of obscene, profane language or gestures." Fraser was suspended from school for two days and removed from the list of students who were eligible to make graduation remarks. His parents appealed the case to the Supreme Court.

In the ensuing case, *Bethel School District v. Fraser* (1986), the Court found, in a 7-2 decision, that it was appropriate for the school to prohibit the use of vulgarity and offensive conduct. The majority opinion argues that "the purpose of public education in America is to teach fundamental values.... These fundamental values...must...include consideration of the political sensibilities of other students." The First Amendment does not prohibit schools from prohibiting vulgar and lewd actions inconsistent with the "fundamental values of public school education."

A. Identify the constitutional clause that is common to both *Bethel School District v. Fraser* (1986) and *Tinker vs Des Moines* (1969).

B. Based on the constitutional clause identified in part A, explain why the facts of *Bethel School District v. Fraser* (1986) led to a different holding than the holding of *Tinker vs Des Moines* (1969).

C. Describe a political action that individuals could take to prevent another incident similar to the circumstances of *Bethel School District v. Fraser* (1986).

Exemplary Answer

A. *The constitutional issue in common to both the* Fraser *and* Tinker *cases is the freedom of speech protection in the First Amendment.*

B. *In* Tinker, *the Supreme Court held that student armbands in protest of the Vietnam War was symbolic speech and the school had not demonstrated that they had disrupted education activities. The armbands are peaceful protest and protected by the Constitution. In* Fraser, *the court held that student's use of vulgar speech did disrupt the purpose and values of public school and was therefore unconstitutional. Speech is limited when it becomes destructive of fundamental values that the public expects schools to follow.*

C. *The school district could prevent incidents similar to* Fraser *by making guidelines on proper use of speech and educating students who wish to exercise their speech rights in school. The district should continue to provide forums for student speech and involve students in educating others on its limits. Administrators could review written copies of student speeches before approving them similar to graduation speeches by the valedictorian and salutatorian.*

Practice Free Response Question: Type 3 – Supreme Court Comparison

Directions: Respond to each part of the question below and separate your answers using the A, B, and C indicators. This FRQ is worth four points based on the breakdown below. You have 20-minutes to complete your answer.

- Part A: identify the similarity between the court cases
- Part B: provide factual information about *Schenck v. United States* (1919)
- Part B: explain how that information is relevant to *Yates v. United States* (1956)
- Part C: describe an interaction between *Yates v. United States* (1956) and the public.

Fourteen leaders of the Communist Party in California, were indicted in 1951 under the Smith Act for conspiring to teach the overthrowing of the U.S. government by force and violence, and to organize the Communist Party of the U.S. to support it. The leaders were convicted after a jury trial, and their convictions were sustained by the Court of Appeals. Yates claimed that the Communist Party was engaged in passive political activities and that any violation of the Smith Act must involve active attempts to overthrow the government.

In the ensuing case, *Yates v. United States* (1956), the Supreme Court overturned the Communist leaders' convictions in a 6-1 decision. The majority argued that the Smith Act did not prohibit "advocacy of forcible overthrow of the government as an abstract doctrine." The Court drew a distinction between the "teaching of forcible overthrow as an abstract principle" and the "teaching of concrete action for the forcible overthrow of the Government."

A. Identify the constitutional clause that is common to both *Yates v. United States* (1956) and *Schenck v. United States* (1919).

B. Based on the constitutional clause identified in part A, explain why the facts of *Schenck v. United States* (1919) led to a different holding than the holding in *Yates v. United States* (1956).

C. Describe an action that members of the public who disagree with the holding in *Yates v. United States* (1956) could take to limit its impact.

Exemplary Answer

A. *The constitutional issue in common to both the* Schenck *and* Yates *cases is the freedom of speech protection in the First Amendment.*

B. *In* Schenck, *the Supreme Court held that speech representing a "clear and present danger" is not protected by the First Amendment. Schenck's speech directly obstructed the military draft during a time of war. However, in* Yates, *the court held that teaching communism, even though it advocates the overthrow of a democratic and capitalist system like the U.S., is protected speech under the First Amendment. Yates' teaching did not represent a "clear and present danger" of an active attempt to overthrow the U.S. government.*

C. *Members of the public could organize an interest group to counter the Communist Party's political activities. The community obviously has strong beliefs against communism and has significant financial resources. Members of the public had to spend at least hundreds of thousands of dollars on lawyers and court fees to oppose communism in the courts. Instead, financial resources could sponsor Young Democrat and Young Republican conferences that provide access to patriotic politicians and promote public speakers who can describe the limitations of living under communist rule.*

Practice Free Response Question: Type 3 – Supreme Court Comparison

Directions: Respond to each part of the question below and separate your answers using the A, B, and C indicators. This FRQ is worth four points based on the breakdown below. You have 20-minutes to complete your answer.

- Part A: identify the similarity between the court cases
- Part B: provide factual information about *Schenck v. United States* (1919)
- Part B: explain how that information is relevant to *Black v. Virginia* (2003)
- Part C: describe an interaction between *Black v. Virginia* (2003) and the public.

On August 22, 1998 Barry Black led a Ku Klux Klan rally in Carroll Country, Virginia. There, he burned a cross on private property with permission of the owner. Black and two friends were convicted under a Virginia law that banned cross burning with the intention of creating fear in a person or group. Black's action was taken as evidence of such an intention.

In the ensuing case, *Black v. Virginia* (2003), the Supreme Court held in a 7-2 decision that the Virginia law was unconstitutional. The majority opinion stated that while a state may ban cross burning carried out with the intent to intimidate, Virginia's prosecution treated any cross burning as evidence of intimidation. Therefore, the law as written was not enforceable. However, cross-burning can be a criminal offense if the intent to intimidate is proven.

A. Identify the constitutional clause that is common to both *Virginia v. Black* (2003) and *Schenck v. United States* (1919).

B. Based on the constitutional clause identified in part A, explain why the facts of *Schenck v. United States* led to a different holding than the holding in *Virginia v. Black*.

C. Describe an action that members of the public who disagree with the holding in *Virginia v. Black* could take to limit its impact.

Exemplary Answer

A. *The constitutional issue in common to both the* Schenck *and* Black *cases is the freedom of speech protection in the First Amendment.*

B. *In* Schenck, *the Supreme Court held that speech representing a "clear and present danger" is not protected by the First Amendment. Schenck's speech was intended to disrupt the military draft during a time of war. However, in* Black, *the court held that burning a cross on private property did not represent a clear danger of intimidation. Although Black's action was not popular, his freedom of speech is protected because it was not directly aimed at a specific person or group.*

C. *The people of Virginia unhappy with the* Black *decision, could bring strong media attention to the activities of the local KKK group. They could host rallies that celebrate diversity. Leaders of KKK opposition groups could publish the names of Klan members and organize boycotts of businesses that hire or are owned by KKK members. Exposure is sometimes the best strategy to isolate ideas and limit their spread in the community.*

Practice Free Response Question: Type 3 – Supreme Court Comparison

Directions: Respond to each part of the question below and separate your answers using the A, B, and C indicators. This FRQ is worth four points based on the breakdown below. You have 20-minutes to complete your answer.

- Part A: identify the similarity between the court cases
- Part B1: provide factual information about *New York Times v. U.S.* (1971)
- Part B2: explain how that information is relevant to *Hazelwood School District v. Kuhlmeier* (1988)
- Part C: describe an interaction between *Hazelwood School District v. Kuhlmeier* (1988) and the public

Students enrolled in the Journalism II class at Hazelwood East High School submitted two articles for publication containing stories on divorce and teenage pregnancy. The school principal felt that the subjects of these two articles were inappropriate. He concluded that journalistic fairness required that the father in the divorce article be informed of the story and be given an opportunity to comment. He also stated his concerns that simply changing the names of the girls in the teenage pregnancy article may not be sufficient to protect their anonymity and that this topic may not be suitable for the younger students. As a result, he prohibited these articles from being published in the paper.

The U.S. Supreme Court held in a 5-3 vote that the principal's actions did not violate the students' rights. The paper was sponsored by the school and the principal had a legitimate interest in preventing the publication of articles that it deemed inappropriate and that might appear to have the approval of the school. The Court noted that the paper was not intended as a public forum in which everyone could share views; rather, it was a limited forum for journalism students to write articles pursuant to the requirements of their Journalism II class, and subject to appropriate editing by the school.

A. Identify the constitutional clause that is common to both *Hazelwood School District v. Kuhlmeier* (1988) and *New York Times v. U.S.* (1971).

B. Based on the constitutional clause identified in part A, explain why the facts of *New York Times v. U.S.* (1971) are different than the holding of *Hazelwood School District v. Kuhlmeier* (1988).

C. Describe a political action that individuals could take to prevent another situation like the *Hazelwood* case (1988).

Exemplary Answer

A. *The constitutional issue in common to both the* New York Times *and* Kuhlmeier *cases is the freedom of press protection in the First Amendment.*

B. *In* New York Times, *the Supreme Court held that the First Amendment protects the press against "prior restraint" by the government, even in cases involving national security. However, in* Kuhlmeier, *the court held that the principal was doing his duty by restraining the publication of articles in the school newspaper that would be embarrassing to students and parents. School authorities have the right to review articles before publication because they have a duty to represent the community standard. The community standard has precedence over student freedom of press.*

C. *For high school students and their parents to take a student publication issue to the Supreme Court means that the community has a strong interest in promoting student speech and interest in journalistic and legal issues. The community (school, city council, interest group) could sponsor journalism students and their parents to attend a professional media conference. There, they are can learn about libel issues and limits on freedom of speech. Leaders in the community can help educate students by connecting them with professionals. Local journalists could be invited to a Q&A session after school so that the community can become better informed on legal responsibilities.*

Practice Free Response Question: Type 3 – Supreme Court Comparison

Directions: Respond to each part of the question below and separate your answers using the A, B, and C indicators. This FRQ is worth four points based on the breakdown below. You have 20-minutes to complete your answer.
- Part A: identify the similarity between the court cases
- Part B1: provide factual information about *McDonald v. Chicago* (2010).
- Part B2: explain how that information is relevant to *United States v. Miller* (1939)
- Part C: describe an interaction between *United States v. Miller* (1939) and Congress.

An Arkansas federal district court charged Jack Miller and Frank Layton with violating the National Firearms Act of 1934 (NFA) when they transported a sawed-off double-barrel 12-gauge shotgun in interstate commerce without having registered it and without having in his possession a stamp-affixed written order for it, as required by the Act. Miller and Layton argued that possession was a protected right for self-defense. The district court agreed and dismissed the case.

However, the Supreme Court reversed the district court in *United States v. Miller* (1939). In an 8-0 decision, the majority opinion held that the purpose of the Constitution was to maintain effective state militias. Therefore, Congress can require registration of a 12-gauge sawed-off shotgun if carried across state lines. Miller's possession does not contribute to the preservation of a state militia.

A. Identify the constitutional clause that is common to both *United States v. Miller* (1939) and *McDonald v. Chicago* (2010).

B. Based on the constitutional clause identified in part A, explain why the facts of *McDonald v. Chicago* (2010) are different than the holding of *United States v. Miller* (1939).

C. Describe an action that the U.S. Congress can take to prevent judicial activism based on the *McDonald* holding (2010).

Exemplary Answer

A. *The constitutional issue in common to both the* McDonald *and* Miller *cases is the right to bear arms protection of the Second Amendment.*

B. *In* McDonald, *the Supreme Court held that the right to bear arms applies to the city of Chicago through the due process clause of the Fourteenth Amendment. The city's refusal to allow McDonald a gun registration was unconstitutional. McDonald has a right to self-protection. In* Miller, *the court held that the case was not about gun registration. Requiring registration was constitutional. The issue was whether sawed off shotguns contributed to the protection of an armed citizenry – the purpose of the Second Amendment.*

C. *Congress can pass legislation that specifies which type of weapons are considered "contributions to the preservation of a state militia." Congress has the expressed power to determine punishments for violations of the law and can also regulate interstate commerce in gun sales to limit the market for weapons that do not meet the "state militia" standard.*

Practice Free Response Question: Type 3 – Supreme Court Comparison

Directions: Respond to each part of the question below and separate your answers using the A, B, and C indicators. This FRQ is worth four points based on the breakdown below. You have 20-minutes to complete your answer.

- Part A: identify the similarity between the court cases
- Part B1: provide factual information about *Gideon v. Wainwright*
- Part B2: explain how that information is relevant to *Escobedo v. Illinois* (1964)
- Part C: describe an interaction between *Escobedo v. Illinois* (1964) and a legal process.

Danny Escobedo's brother-in-law was shot and killed on the night of January 19, 1960. Escobedo was arrested without a warrant early the next morning and interrogated. Escobedo declined and asked to speak to his attorney, but the police refused, explaining that although he was not formally charged yet, he was in custody and could not leave. His attorney went to the police station and repeatedly asked to see his client and was repeatedly refused access. Police interrogated Escobedo for over fourteen hours and continued to refuse his request for an attorney. Escobedo was not advised of his right to remain silent before the interrogation. While being questioned, Escobedo made statements indicating his knowledge of the crime. After conviction for murder, Escobedo appealed the ruling.

In the ensuing case, *Escobedo v. Illinois* (1964), the Supreme Court held in a 5-4 decision that Escobedo's incriminating statements must not be admitted into evidence. A law enforcement system that relies too much on a confession is more subject to abuses than one that depends on evidence obtained through skillful investigation. The result recognizes this idea.

A. Identify the constitutional clause that is common to both *Escobedo v. Illinois* (1964) and *Gideon v. Wainwright* (1963).

B. Based on the constitutional clause identified in part A, explain why the facts of *Gideon v. Wainwright* (1963) extended the holding that was found in *Escobedo v. Illinois* (1964).

C. Describe a process today that prevents situations similar to the *Escobedo* from occurring.

Exemplary Answer

A. *The constitutional issue in common to both the* Escobedo *and* Gideon *cases is the right to counsel protection in the Sixth Amendment.*

B. *In* Gideon, *the Supreme Court held that the state must guarantee the poor a right to an attorney. Without one, citizens do not receive a fair trial. Gideon was refused an attorney. In Escobedo, the court held that interrogations without an attorney present can be inadmissible evidence. Escobedo had an attorney but was denied access to him until after a long interrogation and written statement.*

C. *Today, law enforcement must read accused citizens under criminal interrogation their Miranda rights. These rights inform citizens they can remain silent and they have the right to have an attorney present. Today, law enforcement cannot use any evidence obtained illegally (no search warrant, no permission, no lawyer present) against the accused. This is called the exclusionary rule and would have prevented Escobedo's statement from being used against him in court.*

Practice Free Response Question: Type 3 – Supreme Court Comparison

Directions: Respond to each part of the question below and separate your answers using the A, B, and C indicators. This FRQ is worth four points based on the breakdown below. You have 20-minutes to complete your answer.

- Part A: identify the similarity between the court cases
- Part B1: provide factual information about *Roe v. Wade* (1973)
- Part B2: explain how that information is relevant to *Bowers v. Hardwick* (1986)
- Part C: describe an interaction between *Bowers v. Hardwick* (1986) and the public

Michael Hardwick was observed by a Georgia police officer while engaging in the act of consensual homosexual sodomy with another adult in the bedroom of his home. After being charged with violating a Georgia law that criminalized sodomy, Hardwick challenged the statute's constitutionality. He argued that the anti-sodomy law placed him in imminent danger of arrest. A divided federal court found that there was no constitutional protection for acts of sodomy, and that states could outlaw those practices.

The U.S. Supreme Court held in a 5-4 that there was no constitutional protection for acts of sodomy, and that states could outlaw those practices. The majority opinion argued that the Court has acted to protect rights not easily identifiable in the Constitution only when those rights are "implicit in the concept of ordered liberty" or when they are "deeply rooted in the nation's history and tradition." The Court held that the right to commit sodomy did not meet either of these standards. The majority feared that guaranteeing a right to sodomy would be the product of "judge-made constitutional law" and send the Court down the road of illegitimacy.

A. Identify the constitutional clause that is common to both and *Roe v. Wade* (1973) and *Bowers v. Hardwick* (1986).

B. Based on the constitutional clause identified in part A, explain why the facts of *Roe v. Wade* (1973) are different than the holding of *Bowers v. Hardwick* (1986).

C. Describe an action that individuals who disagreed with the *Bowers v. Hardwick* (1986) could take to change the impact of the decision.

Exemplary Answer

A. *The constitutional issue in common to both the* Roe *and* Hardwick *cases is the right to privacy assumed to be part of the Ninth Amendment.*

B. *In* Roe, *the Supreme Court held that the Ninth Amendment "right to privacy" extend to a woman's decision to have an abortion. Women and families have a right to privacy in their decisions about having children. But these rights are not absolute and can be limited by law. However, in* Johnson, *the court held that the right to privacy did not extend to sexual relationships that are not a deeply-rooted tradition or implicit in the meaning of personal liberty. The state can regulate sodomy as a social standard.*

C. *LGBTQ activists could become more vocal in convincing legislatures and courts to view sodomy as an a socially-acceptable tradition. Achieving this status is essential to overturning the* Hardwick *decision. Interest groups and community activists could encourage LGBTQ legislators and judges to go public with their sexual decisions to demonstrate that policymakers are violating the laws they are sworn to protect.*

Practice Free Response Question: Type 3 – Supreme Court Comparison

Directions: Respond to each part of the question below and separate your answers using the A, B, and C indicators. This FRQ is worth four points based on the breakdown below. You have 20-minutes to complete your answer.

- Part A: identify the similarity between the court cases
- Part B: describe factual information about *Brown v. Board* (1954)
- Part B: then explain how that information is relevant to *University of California v. Bakke* (1978)
- Part C: describe an interaction between *University of California v. Bakke* (1978) and the states.

Allan Bakke, a white California man who had twice unsuccessfully applied for admission to the medical school, filed suit against the university. Citing evidence that his grades and test scores surpassed those of many minority students who had been accepted for admission, Bakke charged that he had suffered unfair "reverse discrimination" on the basis of race, which he argued was contrary to the Civil Rights Act of 1964. The University argued that 16 places in the class of 100 were reserved for minorities as an affirmative action strategy to ensure a diverse student population.

In the ensuing case, *University of California v. Bakke* (1978), the Supreme Court held in an 8–1 decision that affirmative action in college admissions was constitutional, but that racial quotas like those used by the University of California at the time, were not. The court ordered that the medical school admit Bakke, but it also contended that race could be used as one criterion in the admissions decisions of institutions of higher education. Although the ruling legalized the use of affirmative action, in subsequent decisions during the next several decades the court limited the scope of such programs, and several U.S. states prohibited affirmative action programs based on race.

A. Identify the constitutional clause that is common to both *University of California v. Bakke* (1978) and *Brown v. Board* (1954).

B. Based on the constitutional clause identified in part A, explain why the facts of *Brown v. Board* (1954) led to a similar holding as *University of California v. Bakke* (1978).

C. Describe an action that states could take to address the court's holding in *University of California v. Bakke* (1978)

Exemplary Answer

A. *The constitutional issue in common to both the* Bakke *and* Brown *cases is the equal protection clause of the Fourteenth Amendment.*

B. *In* Brown, *the Supreme Court held that race-based school segregation violates the equal protection clause. Separate-but-equal education is not equal at all. Separating races by definition implies that one is superior to another. Governments cannot claim to make these decisions and uphold equal protection under the law. In* Bakke, *the court held that while race can be used as a criterion to admit students to college it cannot separate students by racial classification. Racial quotas also violate the equal protection clause.*

C. *States can make public university admissions changes so that race is one factor in the decision process. Race can be used to justify the goal of creating a diverse student population during each admissions cycle. Affirmative action now has a long tradition in policymaking that has been accepted by federal courts. As long as students are not primarily separated or identified by race, this factor can be used when many students meet the minimum qualifications to apply.*

UNIT 4: AMERICAN POLITICAL IDEOLOGIES AND BELIEFS

Enduring Understanding METHODS OF POLITICAL ANALYSIS-1: Citizen beliefs about government are shaped by the intersection of demographics, political culture, and dynamic social change.

A. Explain the relationship between core beliefs of U.S. citizens and attitudes about the role of government.
   1. Different interpretations of core values, including individualism, equality of opportunity, free enterprise, rule of law, and limited government, affect the relationship between citizens and the federal government and the relationships citizens have with one another.

B. Explain how cultural factors influence political attitudes and socialization.
   1. Family, schools, peers, media, and social environments (including civic and religious organizations) contribute to the development of an individual's political attitudes and values through the process of political socialization.

   Commentary: Political socialization is the process of acquiring personal political orientations." Most political learning and behavior is based on informal learning – the traditions and beliefs of family, friends, and local culture. The majority of young people will vote based on the political preferences of their parents. In early adulthood, the mass media replaces parents as the main source of political information.

   2. As a result of globalization, U.S. political culture has both influenced and been influenced by the values of other countries.

   3. Generational and lifecycle effects also contribute to the political socialization that influences an individual's political attitudes.

4. The relative importance of major political events in the development of individual political attitudes is an example of political socialization.

Enduring Understanding METHODS OF POLITICAL ANALYSIS-2: Public opinion is measured through scientific polling, and the results of public opinion polls influence public policies and institutions.

A. Describe the elements of a scientific poll.
1. Public opinion data that can impact elections and policy debates is affected by such scientific polling types and methods as:
   - **Type of poll**
     - **Opinion polls**: interviews or surveys with samples of citizens that estimate the feelings and beliefs of the entire population
     - **Benchmark or tracking polls**: Continuous surveys that enable a campaign or news organization to chart a candidate's daily rise or fall in support
     - **Entrance polls:** gained popularity during the 2008 caucuses; asked voters about which candidate they are going to vote for and why, before they vote.
     - **Exit polls:** election-related questions asked of voters immediately after they vote. The most popular form of polling used by the mass media to predict the outcome of an election on Election Day.

   - **Sampling techniques**
     - A random sample gives each person in a group the same chance of being selected.
     - In a stratified sampling, the population is divided into sub-groups and weighted based on demographic characteristics of the national population.
     - A mass survey can measure public opinion by interviewing a large sample of the population.
     - A focus group consists of a small number of voters chosen by a political campaign for their demographic similarities who are brought together to determine how the group they represent feels about the candidate.
     - Sampling error: the level of confidence in the findings of a public opinion poll. The more people interviewed, the more confident one can be of the results. Most political polls include a sample of 1000 respondents with an error under 5 percent.

B. Explain the quality and credibility of claims based on public opinion data.
1. The relationship between scientific polling and elections and policy debated is affected by the:
   - Importance of public opinion as a source of political influence in a given election or policy debate: Pollsters argue that polling is a *tool for democracy* where policymakers can keep in touch with changing opinions. Critics argue that polling is often so biased they cannot be assumed to reflect the will of the people. They also contend that poll data on personality attributes and feelings toward candidates overshadows the issues of policy making.

Enduring Understanding COMPETITING POLICY-MAKING INTERESTS-4: Widely held political ideologies shape policy debates and choices in American policies.

A. Explain how the ideologies of the two major parties shape policy debates.
1. The Democrat Party platform generally align more closely to liberal ideological positions, and the Republican Party platforms generally align more closely to conservative ideological positions.

B. Explain how U.S. political culture (e.g., values, attitudes, and beliefs) influences the formation, goals, and implementation of public policy over time.
1. Because the U.S. is a democracy with a diverse society, public policies generated at any given time reflect the attitudes and beliefs of citizens who choose to participate in politics at that time.

2. The balancing dynamic of individual liberty and government efforts to promote stability and order has been reflected in policy debates and their outcomes over time.

C. Describe different political ideologies regarding the role of government in regulating the marketplace.
1. Liberal ideologies favor more governmental regulation of the marketplace, conservative ideologies favor fewer regulations, and libertarian ideologies favor little or no regulation of the marketplace beyond the protection of property rights and voluntary trade.

D. Explain how political ideologies vary on the government's role in regulating the marketplace.

1. Ideological differences on marketplace regulation are based on different theoretical support, including Keynesian and supply-side positions on monetary and fiscal policies promoted by the president, Congress, and the Federal Reserve.

- **Fiscal policy** refers to the efforts of the federal government (mostly Congress) to keep the economy stable by increasing or decreasing taxes or government spending. Congress expands the economy by increasing government purchases of goods and services, a decrease in net taxes, or some combination of the two. The U.S. government runs a budget deficit when the government spends more money than it collects in taxes. For fiscal 2018, the U.S. budget deficit was $750 billion. As of 2019, total government debt (the national debt) is $21.5 trillion.

- **Monetary policy** refers to the influence of the Federal Reserve, the nation's central bank, on the amount of money and credit in the U.S. economy. Central banks are often insulated from domestic political pressures and are better able to impose economic restraint. In general, the Federal Reserve expands the economy by purchasing U.S. bonds (debt).

- **Keynesian economics** (also called demand-side economics) refers to increased government spending and tax cuts to raise demand for goods and services.

- **Supply-side economics** focuses on tax cuts and deregulation to improve the economy's ability to produce and supply more output.

E. Explain how political ideologies vary on the role of the government in addressing social issues.
1. Liberal ideologies tend to think that personal privacy – areas of behavior where government should not intrude –extends further than conservative ideologies do (except in arenas involving religious and educational freedom); conservative ideologies favor less government involvement to ensure social and economic equality; and libertarian ideologies disfavor any governmental intervention beyond the protection of private property and individual liberty.

F. Explain how different ideologies impact policy on social issues.
1. Policy trends concerning the level of governmental involvement in social issues reflect the success of conservative or liberal perspectives in political parties.

Issue	Liberal	Conservative	Libertarian
Foreign Policy	Less willing to commit troops to action, such as the war with Iraq and defending Afghanistan	Maintain "peace through strength"; more likely to support military intervention around the world	Stop nation building and being policeman throughout world. Peace through trade and diplomacy
Social Policy	Supports affirmative action for minorities; supports gay marriage	Opposes affirmative action; marriage is between a man and a woman; supports "right to life"	Protect personal privacy; opposed to Patriot Act; people should marry whomever they want; legalize marijuana
Economic Policy	Views government as a regulator in the public interest; favors increase in taxes on the rich; favors increased spending on the poor	Favors free-market solutions; advocates low taxes; increased military spending; reign in welfare programs	Supports entrepreneurship, small business, end to property tax; balanced budgets; government spending is largely wasteful
Crime	Invest in prevention programs and rehabilitation to reduce crime	Enact strict consequences for criminals and apply the law to everyone	Crime should be limited to actions of force or fraud. End the War on Drugs. Prisons should be safe, clean, and humane

Practice Free Response Question: Type 2 – Quantitative Analysis

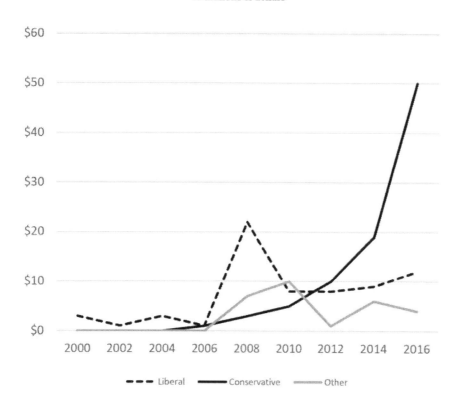

501(c) Spending by Political Viewpoint, 2000–2016
in millions of dollars

Use the graph to answer the questions.

A. Identify the ideology most advantaged by 501(c) spending.

B. Describe a similarity or difference in 501(c) spending by political ideology and draw a conclusion about that similarity or difference.

C. Explain how 501(c) spending as shown in the graph demonstrates free speech.

Exemplary Answer

A. *Conservative groups held the greatest advantage in receiving 501(c) money between 2010 and 2016.*

B. *The gap in spending by conservative and liberal groups widened significantly after the 2012 election. By 2016, conservative groups outspent liberal groups by approximately $50 billion. This significant difference explains why Republican candidates did well getting their message across to the American voters during the 2016 election. The Republicans took control of the presidency and both houses of Congress.*

C. *The enormous amount of money raised and spent by 501(c) groups demonstrates the effect of the Citizens United Supreme Court case. That decision held that money is speech and cannot be limited as an expression of support for political candidates. After the decision, 501(c)s were created by wealthy individuals and corporations to raise and spend money anonymously.*

Practice Free Response Question: Type 2 – Quantitative Analysis

Budget Projections by Congressional Budget Office, 2018
Data represented as percentage of Gross Domestic Product

| | 2018 | Projected Annual Average | | |
		2019–2028	2029–2038	2039–2048
Revenues				
Individual income taxes	8.2	8.9	10.1	10.7
Payroll taxes	5.9	5.9	6.0	6.0
Corporate income taxes	1.2	1.5	1.4	1.4
Other[a]	1.4	1.2	1.3	1.5
Total Revenues	16.6	17.5	18.8	19.5
Outlays				
Mandatory				
Social Security	4.9	5.5	6.2	6.3
Major health care programs[b]	5.2	6.0	7.4	8.7
Other	2.6	2.5	2.3	2.1
Subtotal	12.6	13.9	15.9	17.2
Discretionary	6.3	5.7	5.4	5.5
Net interest	1.6	2.7	3.6	5.3
Total Outlays	20.6	22.4	24.9	27.9
Deficit	-3.9	-4.9	-6.1	-8.4

Use the graph to answer the questions.

A. Identify the greatest expenditure projected in the federal budget table.

B. Describe a trend in federal budget projections between 2018 and 2040 and draw a conclusion about that trend

C. Explain how the budget projection table demonstrates the importance of fiscal policy.

Exemplary Answer

A. *Major health care programs represent the largest expenditure projected in the federal budget.*

B. *Revenue from corporate income taxes is shown to decline slightly between 2028 and 2048. Since the budget projections were created in 2018 when Republicans controlled the Presidency and both Houses of Congress, the CBO is probably basing the figures on the tax cuts that were passed in 2017. Additional tax cuts are planned by the Republicans. The decline in corporate income taxes cannot be explained by a decrease in business activity since the U.S. economy is expanding at a high rate. Individual income taxes are expected to increase significantly during the same period*

C. *The federal government influences the national economy through collection of revenues and expenditures. Through fiscal policy the federal government upholds it promises to fund mandatory health care programs like Medicare and Social Security retirement plans. In order to do so, the federal government is willing to run larger budget deficits, which only increases the amount of taxpayer dollars on interest payments.*

Practice Free Response Question: Type 4 – Argumentative Essay

Develop an argument that explains which priority – individual liberty or social order – has the greatest influence on political ideologies.

In your essay, you must:
- Present a defensible thesis that responds to the prompt and establishes a line of reasoning.

- Support your thesis with at least TWO pieces of accurate and relevant information:
  - At least ONE piece of evidence must be from one of the following foundational documents:
    - U.S. Constitution/Bill of Rights
    - Declaration of Independence
    - Federalist No. 10
  - Use a second piece of evidence from another foundational document from the list or from your study of the political ideologies and beliefs

- Use reasoning to explain why your evidence supports your thesis

- Respond to an opposing or alternative perspective using refutation, concession, or rebuttal

Annotated Answer

All three major political ideologies today rely on individual liberty to create their philosophy and policy actions. Liberals, conservatives, and libertarians refer to the founding principles written in The Declaration of Independence *and* The Bill of Rights *to encourage Americans to become involved in policy decisions.* **[Thesis]**

The Declaration of Independence *argues that a republic not only rests on the values of individual liberty, but that such freedom granted by God. Liberty is the moral authority that political ideologies use to connect with and inspire Americans and peoples across the world. Liberals promote liberty through nondiscrimination legislation, affirmative action as increasing opportunity for the disadvantaged, and LGBTQ rights. Conservatives promote liberty through the property rights and entrepreneurship. Libertarians argue that individual liberty means a limited government and decriminalization of nonviolent offenses.* **[Relevant evidence 1; supports thesis]** *Each ideology uses the Preamble of the Declaration "we hold these truths to be self-evident ...." to frame their platforms and their speeches. By tying their actions to the Founders' words on individual liberty, they appeal to the loyalty of Americans.* **[Reasoning]**

The Bill of *Rights also supports each ideology's priority for individual liberty. The first ten amendments declare that a respect for individual rights is required in order to have social order. The first amendment lists the most important rights of Americans and all refer to personal freedoms. All three ideologies claim to uphold the standard of the first amendment while arguing different interpretations in the nations courts. Conservatives especially champion the second amendment; libertarians love the tenth; liberal groups fund amicus curiae briefs to defend the first.* **[Relevant evidence 2]**

Yet social order is a value that Americans demand. The passage of the Patriot Act and the Freedom Act restricts individual rights for the sake of national security. Americans are open to relinquish some privacy (phone and data records) for the sake of government protection against terrorism. While there are other examples of legal limits to individual liberties, they are the exception, not the norm. American political ideology is so strongly grounded on this freedom that it attracts immigrants from around the world to live and become educated in our democracy. **[Alternative Perspective]**

UNIT 5: POLITICAL PARTICIPATION

Enduring Understanding METHODS OF POLITICAL ANALYSIS-3: Factors associated with political ideology, efficacy, structural barriers, and demographics influence the nature and degree of political participation.

A. Describe the voting rights protections in the Constitution and in legislation.
1. Legal protections found in federal legislation and the **Fifteenth, Seventeenth, Nineteenth, Twenty-Fourth, and Twenty-Sixth Amendments** relate to the expansion of opportunities for political participation.

Legal protection	Expansion of participation
Fifteenth Amendment (1870)	Guaranteed African Americans the right to vote, but full implementation did not occur until 1965. States used literacy tests with grandfather clauses, white primaries, and poll taxes to prevent African American voting.
Voting Rights Act of 1965	Prohibited any government from using voting procedures that denied a person the vote on the basis of race.
Seventeenth Amendment (1913)	Called for the direct election of senators by the voters instead of by state legislatures. A major step in reclaiming power from corporate influence over the Senate.
Nineteenth Amendment (1920)	Guaranteed women the right to vote. Before 1920, 30 states had granted women suffrage either by state constitutional amendment or legislation.
Twenty-Fourth Amendment (1964)	Prohibited poll taxes in federal elections. In 1966, the Supreme Court outlawed poll taxes in state elections.
Twenty-Sixth Amendment	Guaranteed the right to vote to citizens 18 years of age and older.

B. Describe different models of voting behavior.
   1. Examples of political models explaining voting behavior include:
      - Rational-choice voting – Voting based on what is perceived to be in the citizen's individual interest.
      - Retrospective voting – Voting to decide whether the party or candidate in power should be re-elected based on the recent past.
      - Prospective voting – Voting based on predictions of how a party or candidate will perform in the future.
      - Party-line voting – Supporting a party by voting for candidates from one political party for all public offices across the ballot.

C. Explain the roles that individual choice and state laws play in voter turnout in elections.
   1. In addition to the impact that demographics and political efficacy can have on voter choice and turnout, structural barriers and type of election also affect voter turnout in the U.S. as represented by:
      - **State voter registration laws**: the U.S. Census Bureau indicates that 21.4 percent of U.S. citizens were not registered to vote in 2014. This large number of individuals who remain unregistered have spurred major reforms intended to increase voter registration. Most notably, the federal government's National Voter Registration Act of 1993 (NVRA) requires that states allow eligible citizens to register to vote when completing other transactions at state motor vehicle and social services agencies, known as Motor Voter. Oregon became the first state to implement automatic voter registration in 2016. Other states offer Same Day Registration, which allows individuals to register and vote on Election Day, often right at their polling places.

      - **Mid-term (congressional) or general presidential elections**
        Commentary: Political scientists disagree on what explains the significant difference between voter turnout in mid-term election and presidential elections. One theory holds that a surge of interest and information in presidential elections works to the advantage of one party or the other; one party's voter base becomes more likely to vote, while those of the disadvantaged party are more likely to stay home during presidential elections. Midterm elections lack a "wow" factor equivalent to the national media attention given to presidential races. Other political scientists argue that during mid-term elections, the president suffers a "penalty," as voters express dissatisfaction with the president's performance.

U.S. National Voter Turnout, 1789-2014

Source: Vital Statistics of American Politics (CQ Press, Stanley and Niemi, eds.), 2014.

2. Demographic characteristics and political efficacy or engagement are used to predict the likelihood of whether an individual will vote.

   Commentary: Traditionally, groups most likely to vote include: people age 60 and older; whites, African-Americans, the wealthy, and the college-educated. Groups with historically lower voter turnout rates include: people under the age of 30, Hispanics, and adults without a high school diploma;

3. Factors influencing voter choice include:
   - Party identification and ideological orientation
   - Candidate characteristics
   - Contemporary political issues
   - Religious beliefs or affiliation, gender, race and ethnicity, and other demographic characteristics

Enduring Understanding COMPETITING POLICY-MAKING INTERESTS-5: Political parties, interest groups and social movements provide opportunities for participation and influence how people relate to governments and policy-makers.

A. Describe linkage institutions.

1. Linkage institutions are channels, such as the following, that allow individuals to communicate their preferences to policy makers.

   - **Parties** link citizens to candidates running for office. Parties perform three main functions. They select candidates and connect voters to them through campaign activities (voter mobilization, funding candidates); they provide information to voters about the candidates running for office (mailings, party platforms); they gather information about voters for use by candidates and policymakers (voting records, income levels, demographics).

   - **Interest Groups** are organizations of people with similar policy goals that influence the political process to achieve them. Interest groups may support candidates for office, but they do not run their own slate of candidates. Interest groups are policy specialists; they do not try to appeal to everyone. Many interest groups form Political Action Committees (PACs) to raise and spend money to advocate their interests with policymakers. Interest groups use the following strategies to link their members with government decision-makers: petitions, lobbying, grassroots organization, litigation, media campaigns, information dissemination through media.

   - **Elections** are the most direct way that citizens connect with government institutions. They encourage the people to be active in public policy and depend highly on large voter turnout.

   - **Media** act as important linkage institutions between the people and their policymakers. Some political scientists argue that the media serves a "watchdog" role, exposing the actions of officeholders to the American public. The rise of television has encouraged candidates to spend millions of dollars to appeal directly to the people. As a result, political parties have declined and the perceived personalities of the candidates have become a dominant factor in elections. Candidates manipulate the media through scripted media events: press conferences, 30-second TV ads, media releases, and White House briefings. The media's decisions to cover or to ignore certain issues affect public opinion. By focusing public attention on specific problems, the media, however, influence the way in which the public prioritizes issues and how they evaluate politicians. Specifically, the media connects policymakers and constituents by: interviewing citizens and officials, reporting government activities, presenting polls, covering protests.

B. Explain the function and impact of political parties on the electorate and governments.

1. The functions and impact of political parties on the electorate and government are represented by:

- **Mobilization and education of voters**

- **Party platforms** are lists of actions which a political party finalizes at their nation convention. The actions are promises that candidates pledge they will do if elected by voters. The actions in the party platform are not binding.

- **Candidate recruitment**

- **Campaign management**: parties support candidates by hiring a campaign manager, research staff, and policy advisers. Parties are involved in hiring pollsters to gauge public reaction to candidate speeches and ads. They hire press secretaries to make sure the messaging in consistent and clear. They create websites to help candidates with communicating clear policy positions.

- **Fundraising**: parties raise money for candidates. Individuals can contribute up to $30,400 per year to a political party. The party can spend $5,000 per House election, $42,600 per Senate election, and an unlimited amount on advertisements for candidates. These contributions are relatively small when compared to the finance system of interest groups, corporations, and wealthy individuals. See the infographic on page 152 for a detailed illustration on how elections are financed.

- **Committee and party leadership systems in legislatures:** After each election, the party that wins the most representatives is designated the "majority" in each house, and the other party is called the "minority." The majority party selects a Speaker of the House and Majority Leader of the Senate who appoint party leaders as chairmen of committees and prioritize bills for consideration during each session.

C. Explain why and how political parties change and adapt.

1. Parties have adapted to candidate-centered campaigns, and their role in nominating candidates has been weakened.

2. Parties modify their policies and messaging to appeal to various demographic coalitions.

3. The structure of parties has been influenced by:

- **Critical elections and regional realignments**: American politics has always been dominated by a two-party system. When one party has held control for a long period of time, historians and political scientists call it a party era. But party eras diminish and their end is marked by a **critical election**, where new issues arise and recreate priorities among the two factions. **A regional realignment** is associated with a national crisis. The Great Depression ushered in the New Deal coalition of Democrat power. A disenchantment with globalism, deindustrialization, and massive trade deficits may be producing a realignment of Midwestern voters to choose Republican majorities.

- **Campaign finance law** has de-emphasized the role of the national parties in funding elections. The rise of **Super PACs** and politically active nonprofits – 501(c)(4)s and 501(c)(6)s – have become a major force in federal elections since 2014. The term "**dark money**" is often applied to this category of political spender because these groups do not have to disclose the sources of their funding.

  Section 501(c)(4) of the U.S. tax code allows the formation of tax-exempt "social welfare organizations," that collect untaxed money and engage in political advocacy without it being their primary mission. Those organizations don't have to report their membership -- meaning that, with some exceptions, they don't have to report who gives them money. Or how they spend that money. After *Citizens United*, the amount of money spent by 501(c)(4) organizations increased dramatically. undisclosed.

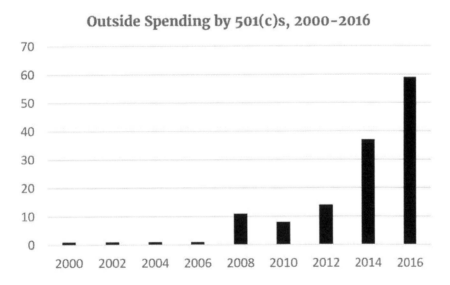

Outside Spending by 501(c)s, 2000-2016

Source: Center for Responsive Politics, 2018

- **Changes in communication and data-management technology**: Some political scientists argue that politics is highly polarized between "liberal" and "conservative" partisanship because technology and demographic data have made it easier (and less risky) for campaigns to target their base instead of appealing to a broad swath of voters. Big data — a combination of massive technological power and endlessly detailed voter information — has changed the way campaigns are conducted. Like corporations, campaigns now know far more about their constituents than ever before — what they read, which movies they stream, which shows they watch, where they shop, which products they buy. This allows campaigns to identify their most likely voters and target them with ads and favorable content. The result is that candidates talk only to voters disposed to agree with them, as opposed to persuading those who don't. Modern campaigns tend to ignore the center and concentrate on the most partisan supporters.

4. Parties use communication technology and voter-data management to disseminate, control and clarify political messages and enhance outreach and mobilization efforts.

D. Explain how structural barriers impact third party and independent candidate success.

1. In comparison to proportional systems, winner-take-all voting districts serve as a structural barrier to third-party and independent candidate success.

2. The incorporation of third-party agendas into platforms of major political parties serves as a barrier to third party and independent candidate success.

- **Winner-take-all system is** an election process where the candidate who receives the most votes wins the election. With single-member congressional districts in the U.S., the **winner-take-all system** allows two major parties to dominate national and state elections.

- In a system that uses **proportional representation** (most European countries), legislative seats are distributed according to each party's percentage of the nationwide vote. A small party may use its seats to combine with one of the larger parties to form a coalition government. In most European countries, parties that achieve a certain small percentage of votes will be awarded seats in the legislature and guarantees that party will be on the ballot of the next election.

- **Importance of third parties**: through American political history, these minor parties have controlled enough votes in one-third of the last 36 presidential elections to have decisively tipped the electoral college vote. In 1992, Ross Perot took away enough votes from George Bush to allow Bill Clinton to win election. In 2000, Ralph Nader took away enough voted from Al Gore to allow George W. Bush to become president. Third parties also bring new groups into the voting population and their positions on issues, if popular enough, are usually adopted by one of the major parties. When this occurs, the minor party declines or ceases to operate.

E. Explain the benefits and potential problems of interest-group influence on elections and policy making.

1. Interest groups may represent very specific or more general interests, and can educate voters and office holders, draft legislation, and mobilize membership to apply pressure on and work with legislators and government agencies.

2. In addition to working within party coalitions, interest groups exert influence through long-standing relationships with bureaucratic agencies, congressional committees, and other interest groups, such relationships are described as "iron triangles" and issue networks and they help interest groups exert influence across political party coalitions.

F. Explain how variation in types of resources of interest groups affects their ability to influence elections and policy making.

1. Interest groups influence may be impacted by:

    - Inequality of political and economic resources

    - Unequal access to decision makers

    - "Free rider" problem is faced by unions and other advocacy groups when people do not join because they can benefit from the groups' activities without officially paying membership dues. The bigger the group, the more serious the problem. To counter this phenomenon, interest groups offer membership benefits travel discounts, free meals at certain restaurants, or free subscriptions to magazines, newspapers, or journals.

G. Explain how various political actions influence public policy outcomes.

1. Single-issue groups, ideological/social movements, and protest movements form with the goal of impacting society and policy making.

2. Competing actors such as interest groups, professional organizations, social movements, the military, and bureaucratic agencies influence policy-making, such as the federal budget process, at key stages and to varying degrees.

3. Elections and political parties are related to major party shifts or initiatives, occasionally leading to political realignments of voting constituencies.

    Commentary: Examples of political realignments include: the 1932 election of Franklin D. Roosevelt and his "New Deal" response to the Great Depression. A coalition of banking and oil industries, city machines, labor unions, blue collar workers, minorities (racial, ethnic and religious), farmers, white Southerners, people on relief, and intellectuals supported Roosevelt in four successive elections and continued to support Democratic candidates until the Civil Rights movement. Another example includes Ronald Reagan's coalition of economic and social conservatives, religious fundamentalists, and anticommunists who rallied behind a conservative ideology of low taxes, deregulation, and large military expenditures. Political scientists argue that Donald Trump has attempted to recreate that coalition to bring the Republican party to dominance in national elections.

In the 2016 election, the Midwestern states (particularly Michigan, Wisconsin, and Pennsylvania) voted Republican instead for the traditional Democrat candidates. The promise of reigniting industry into this region explains the shift in party allegiance. If Republicans fulfill promises of job creation in the Midwest and that party continues to win elections, the region will have experienced a political realignment.

Enduring Understanding CIVIC PARTICIPATION IN A REPRESENTATIVE DEMOCRACY-2: The impact of federal policies on campaigning and electoral rules continues to be contested by both sides of the political spectrum.

A. Explain how the different processes work in a U.S. presidential election.

1. The process and outcome in U.S. presidential elections are impacted by:

   - **Incumbency advantage phenomenon**: the advantage gained by House members after serving more than one term. The advantage has increased over the last few years due to weak party identification, meaning voters are more easily swayed by current representatives of government as long as they exhibit good behavior and can increase opportunities (jobs, industry, building projects) for their constituents. Voters usually support the party of their Congressional preference. This preference can work in favor of a presidential candidate or be a huge barrier to win that district's vote.

   - **Open and closed primaries**: primaries are party nomination elections in each state where voters decide which specific candidate should be the party nominee for each office (president, legislature). In **open primaries**, voters can decide on election day whether they want to participate in the Democratic or Republican contest. In closed primaries, voters must register in advance and declare a party affiliation. Open primaries tend to favor nontraditional candidates by allowing voters to "cross over" and vote for a candidate from a party they generally do not support.

   - **Caucuses** are meetings in congressional districts to determine which candidate delegates from a state party will support. Caucuses are held in small states and usually favor "underdog candidates" who have a strong grassroots election organization.

   - **National Party conventions**: are meetings of the delegates from each state to determine the party's nominee for president. The party convention during presidential election years is nationally televised over four days, promoting the leaders of the party (state, Congressional, and presidential) with speeches, rallies, and the formal selection of the party's presidential candidate.

- **Congressional and State elections** occur every two years. The election cycle between presidential elections are called "Mid-Term Elections" and usually favor the party opposite of the current president. All 435 seats in the House of Representatives are open for election and one-third of the Senate seats are up for election each 2-year cycle.

- **The Electoral College**: consists of popularly elected representatives (or electors) who will formally elect the president and the vice president of the U.S. Rather than directly voting for the President, US citizens vote for the electors. The electors are technically free to vote for anyone eligible to be president but in practice pledge to vote for specific candidates.

B. Explain how the Electoral College impacts democratic participation.

  1. **The Electoral College System** honors the principle of federalism. State electors cast votes for president not the individual voter. If more voters in one state select the Democrat running for president, the Democrat Party in the state will then choose the state electors who will officially cast votes in the Electoral College. In modern elections, most states have a strong tradition of voting Democrat or Republican. States that have a tendency to alternate their choice between the two major parties are called "swing states" and presidential candidates will spend large amounts of time and money to court these voters. Swing states like Colorado, Florida, Ohio, Pennsylvania, North Carolina, Virginia, Nevada, and Wisconsin usually determine the winner of presidential contests. The Electoral College is a winner-take-all allocation of votes per state (except Main and Nebraska).

C. Explain how different processes work in U.S. congressional elections.

  1. The process and outcomes in U.S. Congressional elections are impacted by:

     - Incumbency advantage phenomenon: Since 1982, House incumbents have won 90% of their re-elections; Senate incumbents have won 80%.

     - Open and closed primaries

     - Caucuses

     - General (presidential and mid-term) elections

D. Explain how campaign organizations and strategies affect the election process.

  1. The benefits and drawbacks of modern campaigns are represented by:

     - Dependence on professional consultants

- Rising campaign costs and intensive fundraising efforts: Over one billion dollars was spent by candidates running for President in 2016. The average cost of winning a House seat is $1.7 million; the average cost of winning a Senate seat is $10.5 million.

- Duration of election cycles

- **Impact of and reliance on social media campaigns communication and fundraising**: Brad Parscale, the founder of the Giles-Parscale agency and chief executive of Trump's digital efforts for 2016 and 2020 designed a social media campaign that began with a $2 million investment in Facebook ads. He uploaded the names of Trump supporters first and found them on Facebook. Then he targeted others who had things in common with them, such as activity or demographics. These "Lookalike Audiences" were key to the campaign's success. But other types of content, including tens of thousands of different targeted web pages, also played a role. In total, Trump's digital team generated or created more than 100k+ pieces of unique content. Weeks before the election, Parscale targeted three groups that Hillary Clinton needed to win overwhelmingly (idealistic white liberals, young women and African Americans) with $150 million dollars in Instagram and Facebook advertisements. In total, the Trump campaign spent about $70 million a month in advertisements.

E. Explain how the organization, finance, and strategies of national political campaigns affect the election process.

1. Federal legislation and case law pertaining to campaign finance demonstrate the ongoing debate over the role of money in political and free speech, as set forth in:

   - Bipartisan Campaign Reform Act of 2002, which was an effort to ban soft money and reduce attack ads with "Stand by Your Ad" provision: "I'm [candidate's name] and I approve this message."

   - *Citizens United v. Federal Election Commission* (2010), which ruled that political spending by corporations, associations, and labor unions is a form of protected speech under the **First Amendment.**

Citizens United v. Federal Election Commission (2010)

Constitutional Issue: Freedom of Speech, First Amendment

Question: Does a state law requiring children to attend school until the age of 16 violate Amish rights under the free exercise of religion clause of the First Amendment?

Background

Citizens United is a nonprofit organization with a 12 million budget. Some of its funding comes from for-profit corporations. This organization created a 90-minute documentary named *Hillary*, which names Hillary Clinton and shows interview and political commentators all who urged voters to not vote for her. The organization first released the movie in theaters and then on DVD. Afterwards the organization produced two 10-second ads and one 30-second ad promoting viewers to order the documentary on-demand. A negative statement about Hillary is made and then information on how to find the website is given. This movie is basically a feature-length negative advertisement against Hillary.

However, the 2002 Bipartisan Campaign Reform Act (BCRA) popularly known as McCain-Feingold limited use of corporate or union general treasury funds to support electioneering communications within 30 days of a primary election or 60 days of a general election. The terms of the BCRA specifically limited communications that mentioned candidates by name and were widely distributed. Fearful of potential liability, Citizens United brought suit against the FEC arguing that the limitations of the BCRA were unconstitutional as applied to the film in question.

Holding and Reasoning

Political spending by corporations, associations, and labor unions is a form of protected speech under the First Amendment.

In a 5-4 decision, the U.S. Supreme Court tossed out the corporate and union ban on making independent expenditures and financing electioneering communications. It gave corporations and unions the green light to spend unlimited sums on ads and other political tools, calling for the election or defeat of individual candidates. Corporations and labor unions can spend as much as they want to convince people to vote for or against a candidate. Spending is speech and is therefore protected by the Constitution — even if the speaker is a corporation. The decision did not affect contributions. It is still illegal for companies and labor unions to give money directly to candidates for federal office. The court said that because these funds were not being spent in coordination with a campaign, they "do not give rise to corruption or the appearance of corruption."

2. Debates have increased over free speech and competitive and fair elections related to money and campaign funding (including contributions from individuals, PACS, and political parties)

3. Different types of political action committees (PACs) influence elections and policy making through fundraising and spending.

Campaign Finance Law

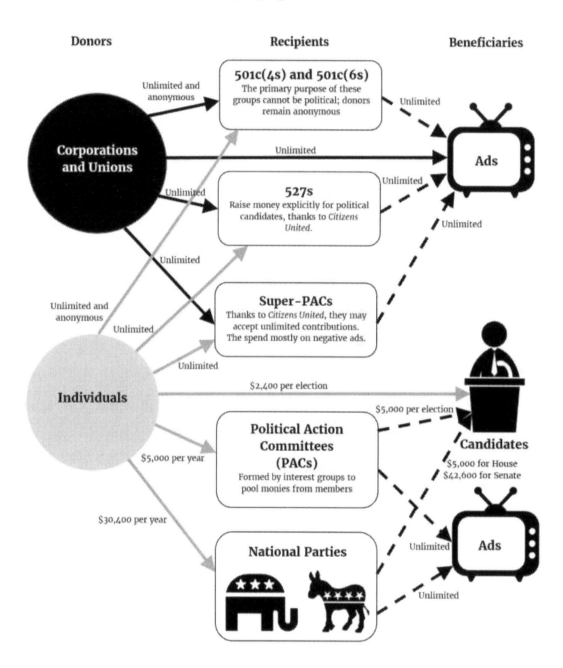

Enduring Understanding CIVIC PARTICIPATION IN A REPRESENTATIVE DEMOCRACY-3: The various forms of media provide citizens with political information in which they participate politically.

A. Explain the media's role as a linkage institution.

    1. Traditional news media, new communication technologies, and advances in social media have profoundly influenced how citizens routinely acquire political information, including new events, investigative journalism, election coverage, and political commentary.

    2. The media's use of polling results to convey popular levels of trust and confidence in government can impact elections by turning such events into "horse races" based more on popularity and factors other than qualifications and platforms of candidates.

B. Explain how increasingly diverse choices of media and communication outlets influence political institutions and behavior.

    1. Political participation is influenced by a variety of media coverage, analysis, and commentary on political events.

    2. The rapidly increasing demand for media and political communications outlets from an ideologically diverse audience have led to debates over media bias and the impact of media ownership and partisan news sites.

    3. The nature of democratic debate and the level of political knowledge among citizens in impacted by:

        • Increased media choices

        • Ideologically oriented programming

        • Consumer-driven media outlets and emerging technologies that reinforce existing beliefs

        • Uncertainty over the credibility of news sources and information

Practice Free Response Question: Type 1 – Concept Application

In April, the Trump administration said it was weighing whether to levy tariffs on more than 1,300 Chinese exports, which included flat-screen televisions, aircraft parts, and medical devices. That would make them more expensive for American consumers and manufacturers. The Trump administration's goal is to hit China's more high-tech exports and damage Beijing's "Made in China 2025" program, a huge state-sponsored initiative to make China a world-class manufacturer of goods like robotics and high-end electronics....

China quickly threatened to respond in kind with tariffs on $50 billion worth of US exports to China, including cars, airplanes, and soybeans. The last one could deal a particularly serious political blow to Trump and his fellow Republicans: The biggest soybean producers in the US include Ohio, Iowa, Missouri, and Indiana — states in the heart of Trump country where neither the president nor his party wants to see economic instability or job losses.

Vox.com, May 29, 2018

After reading the scenario, respond to A, B, and C below.

A. Describe a power the president could use to bring an end to the situation addressed in the scenario.

B. In the context of the scenario, explain how the President's power described in Part A can be affected by its interaction with Congress.

C. In the context of the scenario, explain how the interaction between Congress and the presidency can be affected by a presidential election year.

Exemplary Answer

A. *The president could use his power of treaty or executive agreement to negotiate a long-term trade deal with China. He could also raise tariffs so high on Chinese goods that there would effectively be no imports from that nation.*

B. *Congress has the constitutional power to regulate foreign trade and can pass a law setting tariffs on China that would take precedence over the President's executive actions.*

C. *During a presidential election year, the actions of the president and Congress become tests of approval with the American public. Tariffs protect industries in the United States and would be seen favorably by many big businesses, the companies that serve them, and the employees. Donald Trump and the Republicans won the 2016 elections based on bringing back American industry. If those promises and tariff actions continue to be popular, then members of Congress, both Republicans and Democrats, would have to take a more nationalist position on issues to win election.*

Practice Free Response Question: Type 1 – Concept Application

On Monday, a fringe political group out of California called for the state's central, mostly rural counties to break away from the rest of the state. Organizers gathered in a government building outside Sacramento for a reading of their own Declaration of Independence from California.... New California would be made up of roughly 15 million people across 42 counties, leaving the state's coastal urban enclaves like Los Angeles and San Francisco on their own.

The split would result in, effectively, a blue California and a red California.... [Organizers] told CBS Sacramento that the group has representatives from counties across the state, and it plans to organize over the next 10 to 18 months. Then it will engage the state legislature.

Businessinsider.com, January 17, 2018

After reading the scenario, respond to A, B, and C below.

    A. Describe a power Congress can use to address the proposal described in the scenario.

    B. In the context of the scenario, explain how the proposal, if successful, would alter the structure of Congress.

    C. In the context of the scenario, explain how a successful proposal would affect the next presidential election.

Exemplary Answer

A. *Congress has the power to admit new states and no new state can be created from an exisiting state without their approval.*

B. *If California was divided into two separate states, the seats in the House of Representatives would have to be redistributed based on population, and the Senate would grow by two members when the "new" state gets representation.*

C. *The division of California into a "red" and a "blue" state would significantly affect the next presidential election. California typically chooses the Democrat candidate. If the electoral votes were divided between a majority Republican-leaning state and a majority Democrat-leaning state, the Republican candidate for president would gain a huge advantage, picking up electoral college votes where ordinarily the Democrat candidate receives them all.*

Practice Free Response Question: Type 1 – Concept Application

The Democratic Party's superdelegate system has come under attack this presidential election.... There are hundreds of superdelegates, unelected party delegates, who can sway the election, undermining the candidate democratically chosen by the party's mass base.

Bernie Sanders won the election in New Hampshire by a landslide in early February, with 60 percent of votes to Hillary Clinton's 38 percent. Sanders won every demographic group, excluding rich voters and those aged 65 and older. Yet, although Clinton drastically lost, she ended up leaving with an equal number of delegates. This is because of the superdelegate system.

"Unpledged delegates exist really to make sure that party leaders and elected officials don't have to be in a position where they are running against grassroots activists," Democratic National Chairwoman Debbie Wasserman Schultz explained.

Salon.com, February 13, 2016

After reading the scenario, respond to A, B, and C below.

A. Describe the process in presidential elections addressed in the scenario.

B. In the context of the scenario, explain how the election process described in Part A impacts democratic participation.

C. In the context of the scenario, explain how the election process is an example of a model of representative democracy.

Exemplary Answer

A. *The process of becoming the Democrat candidate for president is called the primary elections.*

B. *When the Democrat party uses unelected superdelegates to choose their nominee, the system dilutes democratic participation. In the example described in the article, candidate Bernie Sanders received the majority votes of the people of New Hampshire, but the state delegates who formally choose the nominee was split evenly between Sanders and Clinton.*

C. *The Democrat Party's system of superdelegates is an example of elite democracy, where, even though citizens can exercise their right to vote, the elite control the decision-making. The Democrat superdelegates represent the established party members such as career politicans, partisan professors, and party leaders instead of the common citizen. This elite form of control guarantees that an "insider" will win the nomination. Many complain that the primary election process is rigged, through superdelegate voting.*

Practice Free Response Question: Type 2 – Quantitative Analysis

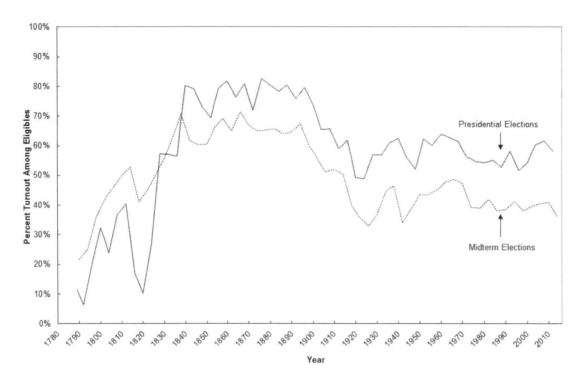

Use the graph to answer the questions.

A. Identify the relationship between voter turnout in presidential elections and voter turnout in midterm elections.

B. Describe a trend or pattern in turnout during presidential elections since 1900 and draw a conclusion about that trend or pattern.

C. Explain what voter turnout as shown in the graph demonstrates about political efficacy.

Exemplary Answer

A. *In the past 100 years, voter turnout in presidential elections is about 20% higher than voter turnout in midterm elections (60% to 40%).*

B. *Since 1900, voter turnout in presidential elections has remained fairly constant at 60%. However, several times during that period, turnout has peaked higer than 60% -- during times of national crisis (Great Depression in the 1930s and Civil Right movement of the 1960s) and also to elect the first African American president in 2008.*

C. *Political efficacy refers to citizens' trust in government – that their participation in voting will be meaningful. The graph demonstrates that people believe their vote is more important in electing presidents rather than their Congressman, probably because the influence of one representative is less consequential in policymaking than the influence of a chief executive.*

Practice Free Response Question: Type 4 – Argumentative Essay

Develop an argument that explains which linkage institution – political parties, interest groups, or media – best supports citizen influence on policy-makers.

In your essay, you must:
- Present a defensible thesis that responds to the prompt and establishes a line of reasoning.

- Support your thesis with at least TWO pieces of accurate and relevant information:
  - At least ONE piece of evidence must be from one of the following foundational documents:
    - U.S. Constitution
    - Federalist No. 10
    - Letter from a Birmingham Jail
  - Use a second piece of evidence from another foundational document from the list or from your study of linkage institutions

- Use reasoning to explain why your evidence supports your thesis

- Respond to an opposing or alternative perspective using refutation, concession, or rebuttal

Annotated Answer

Linkage institutions connect the voice of the people to policymakers. In American politics, interest groups are the most influential on policymaking by <u>initiating</u>, then organizing mass support for policy, especially in amending the constitution. **[Thesis]**

Since the Civil War, interest groups have organized to challenge barriers to participation and especially suffrage. Interest groups have been the critical organization to raise awareness of discrimination and organize constitutional changes that benefit disadvantaged groups. Abolitionists pressured Congress and the states to ratify the 15th Amendment which granted suffrage to African-Americans. Later the women's suffrage movement used the same strategies (creating a national organization with demonstrations, publications, and media awareness) to achieve the right to vote across the nation through the 19th Amendment. The interests of the NAACP and the youth groups financed by teachers' organization resulted in the elimination of the poll tax and the vote for 18 to 20-year-olds, respectively. **[Relevant evidence 1; supports thesis]** *Clearly American politics is celebrated for the power of interest group influence in expanding democracy. The success of one group inspires others.* **[Reasoning]**

Constitutional amendments are rare. Interest groups more commonly support the passage of legislation through grassroots organization, hiring lobbyists to provide legislators with ideas, funds, and expertise. Their endorsement of some candidates such as the power of the NRA or MADD, can sway political candidates to favor legislation that would secure the votes of members. **[Relevant evidence 2]**

The media and political parties are tools of interest groups to influence policy-makers. Interest groups have a greater ability than political parties to raise money and spend it on political candidates. Their Super PACs and 501c(4)s have made winning an election more about appealing to major interest groups then party affiliation. And the media are the main beneficiaries of the campaign funds. Super PACs spend most of their funds on media advertising, especially running negative ads against opponents of their philosophy. As a result, media and parties become partners to interest groups when linking the public and policymakers. **[Alternative Perspective]**

Made in the USA
Columbia, SC
17 September 2023

23007809R00089